MESSAGES FROM THE ANGELS OF TRANSPARENCY

"This is a truly inspirational work as it does not follow the normal path of the angel books, of which we have many, but gives an exhilarating look at life's purpose. It sheds light on the unseen angelic forces that support us in our evolutionary process to help us live a life of meaning, joy and grace. I have been fortunate to meet and work with Gaetano who is an earth angel, guiding people back to their soul's path to truly enjoy life again."
Dr Roy Martina MD, author of the bestseller *Emotional Balance*.

"In this beautiful, inspiring and empowering book and with the integrity gained from his own transformational experiences, healer Gaetano Vivo shares the loving truth of the profound spiritual wisdom that is always available to us when we open our hearts."
Dr Jude Currivan award winning author of *The 8th Chakra, The 13th Step and HOPE*.

"To truly follow your path takes stamina, trust, and often a lot of courage. This book is a testament not only to doing just that, but in sharing his story and the beautiful and profound insights he receives, Gaetano helps to bring about a sense of hope, peace and unity that resonates within our hearts."
Barbara Meiklejohn-Free best selling author of *The Heart of All Knowing*

"For many people questions about their sense of belonging and what the future holds are shrouded in uncertainty. The messages channelled in this book, along with the meditations and direct

i

approach to better emotional well-being offer some very good examples of how we can change our own realities and thereby improve things for all those we touch in our lives. Full of optimism and encouragement."
Joylina Goodings, author of *Your Angel Journey*

"Whenever a book comes out that helps to open our hearts to the joy of being and provide a compass for our own map to the Divine, I am uplifted and inspired with hope for the future. This is just such a book."
Susie Anthony, award winning author of *A Map to God* and founder of The Super Hero Code.

"At a time when many of us seem preoccupied with the latest stock market report or celebrity gossip, it is good to be reminded what life on earth is really about: the awakening of the immortal soul and its joyful reconnection with the Angelic realm. This book gives us this valuable reminder."
Sue Vaughan, author of *Kinangiology: Co-working with the Angels to Heal Emotions*

"This book, that combines the ancient gift of touch and the promise of supreme hope and inspiration when we are truly open to receiving a higher energy, offers a delightful insight into the healing journey of life. A gentle and simple reminder that if we choose, we need never journey alone."
Kate Osborne, writer, editor and publicist of the esoteric and founder of Solarus Ltd

Messages from the Angels of Transparency

Powerful words from Gentle Souls

Messages from the Angels of Transparency

Powerful words from Gentle Souls

Gaetano Vivo

AXIS MUNDI
BOOKS

Winchester, UK
Washington, USA

First published by Axis Mundi Books, 2012
Axis Mundi Books is an imprint of John Hunt Publishing Ltd., Laurel House, Station Approach,
Alresford, Hants, SO24 9JH, UK
office1@o-books.net
www.o-books.com

For distributor details and how to order please visit the 'Ordering' section on our website.

Text copyright: Gaetano Vivo 2011

ISBN: 978 1 84694 974 6

A CIP catalogue record for this book is available from the British Library.

Design: Stuart Davies
Cover image: Kate Osborne

Printed and bound by CPI Group (UK) Ltd, Croydon, CR0 4YY
Printed in the USA by Edwards Brothers Malloy

We operate a distinctive and ethical publishing philosophy in all
areas of our business, from our global network of authors to
production and worldwide distribution.

CONTENTS

To Averil, Gabriella, Rochelle, Patrizia,
Laura, Sabrina and Gaia...
They are my Transparency Angels on Earth.

FOREWORD

MEDICINE FOR THE SOUL

*'There is a growing need for the right approach with the patient...
there is a need for a psychological openness and support, not only
between them but also with the entire medical establishment... This is
one of the most important desires for the patient; not to be left alone
in their suffering and anguish, to have someone there for them who
understands their feelings and help to heal.'*
PROFESSOR DAMASO CAPRIOGLIO - EMERITUS
PROFESSOR AT THE FACULTY OF MEDICINE, PROFESSOR
OF ETHICS, UNIVERSITY OF PARMA.

I write this foreword with great joy and gratitude as the result of
an experience from nearly a decade ago with the philosophy of
Reiki. That is all to do with the almost fortuitous encounter with
my Reiki Master, Gaetano Vivo. I got to know him better in
recent years during extensive discussions and examination of his
studies, his experiences, his cases and his results.

As in all new methods and philosophies that are presented,
there have been many different opinions, sometimes conflicting
or even in opposition. Some of these opinions were superficial,
giving people a distorted view and incorrect information, thus
creating suspicion or bias. There are on the other hand, true
scholars of Reiki, and Masters who, through their long
experience, remain close to the teachings received from their
masters, and with the precise and careful observation of results,
have kept their traditions, roots, the principles and precepts of
this discipline, passing it on to their pupils with intelligence,
honesty, integrity and rationality. Gaetano Vivo is one of them.

As a physician and emeritus professor of medicine I must

emphasize a very important prerequisite: Reiki is not intended as an alternative treatment at odds with more conventional medicine. Especially in the sense the European medical culture means it, this tradition is 2500 years old and is rich of years of history and documented tradition, which had a profound impact in the academic world both European and American. But medicine is universal and equally important is the medical care that three thousand years came from the other half of our world, like Asia (China, India, Japan and Tibet).

For thousands of years they have been teaching us that medicine needs to be analyzed, studied, and interpreted in a holistic manner, i.e. in the study of both body and human soul. Eleanor McKenzie clearly emphasizes in her book the fact that Reiki is a personal and 'holistic' - originating from the word 'hal - ' experience, highlighting that the term 'hal' the already existed in the ancient Anglo-Saxon language, where the term 'hal' meant 'complete', 'sacred' and even 'healthy' - enough to survive in some modern phrases, like 'hallowed' (holy), or 'hale and hearty' (alive and robust). That is why Reiki with this holistic prerogative helps the person who receives it to heal and improve from within.

Even Plato saw the separation of body and soul in the treatment of illness and disease as a big mistake. Body and soul cannot be divided. But this is what doctors these days ignore completely and that is why they are missing so many diseases, they unfortunately will never be able to see the 'Whole'. Plato denounced the great lack of attention by his contemporary scientists towards the soul, to be read as psyche, and toward the individuals as whole.

Richard Smith, director of the British Medical Journal wrote in an editorial titled *Ethics of ignorance* in which he argues the need for every doctor to be aware of his limitations and shortcomings not only personal, but of the science in general and in the discipline that he exerts and that the claim of these shortcomings, rather than being perceived as a weakness becomes a strength on which to base daily practice. 'Scio me nihil scire' (I know that I don't know), said the ancient philosophers. It is now crucial the importance of 'continuing education', the accurate and constant updating for each doctor, but this is not enough. Perhaps the universities do not teach enough one of the most important things: how to establish a professional but heart-felt relationship.

Reiki it is a natural healing method that transmits life force. People who practice Reiki, receive this Energy and channel it through their hands into the body of the patient, balancing the so called 'chakras', the energy gateways that everybody has in the body, and with the self Reiki you can practice this on yourself daily. Physician, heal thyself first! This imperative, or if you want, this invitation and exhortation is perfectly indicated and appropriate for those who wish to practice Reiki.

In November 1984 I had one of the first coronary angioplasty procedures. This technique had been in use for only for a few weeks and mine was the only hospital in Italy where you could receive such a treatment After surgery I was advised to have some rehabilitation, and I joined the cardiac rehabilitation centre run by Dr. Rino Pirelli, Institute Don Gnocchi in Milan, where I learned to use a daily aerobic and energy exercise that I run every day since early in the morning before work, a healthy diet with wholesome natural foods and if possible organically grown, and finally with the psychologist Dr. Crushiron learned the technique of meditation and relaxation 'Autogenic Training'. I applied this technique every day, until, I undertook Reiki.

I understood that Reiki was a holistic therapy: a harmonization of energy, being able to revitalize the body and spirit. Working with the seven chakras, we can restore inner harmony by giving balance to the endocrine glands the sympathetic and parasympathetic nervous system, to the nervous plexus. But alongside these great benefits I have also learned and verified on myself how studying and performing Reiki improves our spiritual understanding in a very easy way so that everyone can learn and be inspired in their life. It gives you also a great possibility to explore your psychological potential and at the same time it is also a very powerful tool for relaxation and general well-being and inner harmony, and this leads to learn how to meditate and be in peace with yourself.

I have learned in time to apply the meditation every morning before getting up without the hassle of listening through headphones. Neurons have stored the message, and feel the energy flow with the same result as I gradually move to a different chakra. Another remarkable peculiarity of this method is that the length of time devoted to meditation, listening to music and Reiki can vary, depending on the time available or if I wake in the middle of the night, or if I'm lying in bed with anxiety or fear or strong emotion, sometimes for health problems not only personal but family members or friends. In each of these cases Reiki restores peace, serenity, tranquility, and then allows me to resume sleep.

I have tried many times to control blood pressure and heart rate, and the situation of high blood pressure and both minimum and maximum heart rate return to normal after a Reiki treatment. I also found that this meditation even leads to 'bradycardia' - the reduction in heart rate. This certainly involves the production of endorphins, the positive stimuli to the vagal plexus with a strong balance between the sympathetic and the parasympathetic system.

To repeat what many Reiki Masters are saying these days, this modality allows the people who practice it to live in the present moment, to dive into the reality of the moment we are experiencing. This is a concept which is present in various philosophies such as Zen or Buddhism: to live in the present moment in full consciousness. At the end of the purification of the seven chakras, there is a moment where you can combine the celestial energy to the earth energy, from that we create a strong and powerful energy of Reiki that comes within us flowing and balancing all the chakras and expanding the aura through those brighter colours. That same energy is the one that allows us to perceive a new world around us that makes us looking beyond ourselves to the people who live in the dark and need to come out and breathe a new way of living.

Some authors, like Patrice Gros, compare the energy of Reiki to the compassion of Buddha, of a supreme nature and genuine spirit. Therefore Reiki rejoining mind, body and spirit can bring you to an excellent state of harmony and at the same time raise our consciousness and thus the goodness, purity and love for others. I wish for a better collaboration between who practice medicine and the culture of Reiki and I hope that this gives an incentive to many to study and apply Reiki in order to transmit a message of love and solidarity to the world around us as. As Mother Theresa said, "It is through us that God loves the world".

Prof. DAMASO CAPRIOGLIO, M.D., D.D.S. was born in Rosignano Monferrato (Al) in 1934 graduated in Medicine and Surgery at University of Turin in 1958, post-graduated in Dentistry at University of Pavia in 1960, post-graduated in Orthodontics at University of Cagliari in 1975, degree of Professor in Dentistry (Rome 1964), assistant Professor in Paediatric Dentistry and Orthodontics at Pavia University from 1965 till 1970, Professor of Paediatric Dentistry at Modena University till 1989, Professor and Chairman Department of Paediatric Dentistry and Director Interceptive Orthodontics at Cagliari University from 1990 till 1993. Professor and Chairman, department of Orthodontics and of postgraduated course in Interceptive Orthodontics and pre and post orthodontic surgery at Parma University from 1993 till November 2004. Now teacher of Ethics And Dental Traumatology University of Parma. Head of Dental research department of Dental Children in Milano since 1977. Editor and Founder of Italian Journal of Paediatric Dentistry from 1990 till 1999 and Associate Editor of European Journal of Paediatric Dentistry from 2000. Author of more than 200 scientific papers, 20 text books and 10 translated text books. Past President of Italian Society of Paediatric Dentistry, Past Vice-President of International Association of Dental Traumatology. Member of A.A.O. E.O.S., S.F.O.D., S.I.D.O., W.F.O., Pierre Fauchard Academy. Her research fields are related to Interceptive Orthodontist, Paediatric Dentistry Dental Traumatology and Estetic Dentistry. Member of RotarY Milano sud. He works more than twenty years in Solidarity for young children in Milano and Cameroun and his hobbies include golf and the history of Dental Medicine.

PREFACE

I have received and taught Reiki for many years. Reiki means 'Universal Energy'. Today we cannot simply just contemplate this word; we must first delete from our minds the misuse of the word. Reiki is not a technique, neither is it a religion or a belief, nor is it a magical practice or part of the occult. Understanding Reiki as 'Universal Energy' or 'Transparency' is to know it as the illumination of the heart. It is 'love' and can transform a mere existence to a life that is complete and profound. Reiki is a gift for those who suffer and vital for the spiritual evolution of humankind.

Using Universal Energy means that we are in charge of something greater than ourselves. It is a personal journey, to be given with humility and total acceptance of life. It teaches us to fly and leads us towards transformation and ultimately it enables us to evolve. Channelling Universal Energy is one of the most beautiful gifts that we can receive and share with others. Universal Energy is compassion, harmony, balance and brings us integrity. It is a path of joy and happiness.

More and more individuals have received the gift to reawaken people's hearts. I thank GOD, who has given me this gift to be among them and I am open to share this beautiful experience. I want to continue to teach Reiki. Reiki or Universal Energy is simply the purest expression of Love that exists for us. Such pure love is transparent; it allows the essence of all things to be visible, beyond illusions. Universal Energy is transparent, just like water and air that seem not to exist but are in fact the most important things; they give us life.

This energy is transparent, like the Angels around us, whom we do not see with our eyes but are there for us every second of our lives. We can feel them, hear them and meet them on our journey. We need only to open our hearts and listen to their beautiful messages. The Universal Energy has given me, like many others, the task to reawaken the consciousness of people to live in simplicity and transparency. This mission is to better comprehend ourselves and others using our hearts. Only by opening our hearts we will be able to awaken into a new reality and prepare a new Earth of light, peace, harmony and brotherhood.

Through Universal Energy we will understand ourselves better and the world around us, so that we will be able to create a better future and for the generations to come. Let's build a better world around us without wars, abandoning indifference and resentment. I believe that only when we 'feel' for the lives of everyone else, will we be able to achieve peace in our hearts and compassion for others. Only when we are able to forgive ourselves and others we will win any 'battles' within and outside of ourselves.

I am but an ordinary man who has received a gift from the Universal Energy enabling me to converse with the Angels and the Spirit Guides around us and with this gift I am tasked to understand their messages and to follow their teachings. I started writing this book two years ago. I wanted to share with others what I had found. I am not sure how, but thanks to this book I have started a long journey of self rediscovery, a personal journey inside myself. In these past two years, in total isolation from my work, my students and my clients, I have come face to face with my 'shadows'; those demons that I have tried all my life to come to terms with without success.

Delving inside, I arrived at the core of the issues that gave birth to my shadows and slowly I am coming up again, finding myself and fuelling my 'flame'. I have hugged that inner child again, that was lonely and in despair, lost in the caverns of my body and my spirit, so that for the first time he has felt love, desire and gratification. By turning back, remembering my past, I have gone forward on my path. I have met new teachers of wisdom who have accompanied me together with my Spiritual Guides and Guardian Angels. They have taken me by the hands and let me fly again. The inner child, now healed from his wounds, can move forward, live in the present and prepare for the 'New World' of the future.

INTRODUCTION

MICHAEL

See, I am sending an Angel before you to protect you on your journey
and lead you safely to the place I have prepared for you.

EXODUS 23:20

We are currently living in an extreme age; risky, in constant flux, but with great potential. Humankind is living in a radical period of fundamental transformation, as we did from 600 to 200BC. During this time came the apparition of great personalities who opened human consciousness: Buddha in India, Socrates in Greece, Lao Tzu in China and the prophets of Israel. All of them said that it was time for humankind to listen to its inner voice; its heart, its sense of intrinsic justice, its thirst for knowledge and to forego past dogmas. They said to fight evil, follow goodness and seek the truth that resides within humankind itself. It was a moment of extraordinary evolution and today it is happening once more.

It is again the 'Age of Archangel Michael'; the re-awakening to the conscience of the 'inner light'. This light, this expression of pure love must become like a lighthouse guiding us away from all distractions. This distraction, this uproar has manifested itself into suffering; suffering of planet Earth in all its complexities, the equilibrium of the environment, the harmony of humanity and creation are in crisis. This creates pressure, putting all things under a great deal of stress, causing anxiety and 'new' illnesses, like depression and cancer. Archangel Michael's task is to show humankind the reality of love and the morality of the pure strength of light that we all have inside. His call can be trauma-tizing, waking us from a deep sleep full of nightmares into which humanity periodically falls. Archangel Michael does all this with complete transparency, seeing through the layers and beyond the material limits of existence, feeling the spiritual essence. In the past Michael appeared directly, inspired the prophets and participated in the life of Jesus and the Christian Church. He has been humanized like a saint, and is the third in the celestial hierarchy after God and The Virgin Mary.

Today, in the age of Science, Politics and Economic Power, it seems like Michael has almost disappeared and hidden away, but he continues his job to open the eyes of the blind and the hearts of the poor to fight against evil and the shadow-self. Archangel Michael does this without violence and with a great light in his heart. He opens the minds and the hearts of the men to protect nature and those natural places in which, he has appeared and where there are churches and chapels built to honour his name. For centuries he has worked throughout these sacred sites and he, as a healer, has re-awakened profound spirituality in many who have been searching for teachings that would bring about peace on Earth.

One of these great reformers was Mikhail Gorbaciov. He had to fight against evil in his own country in order to avoid a third world war. He did it through the policy he called 'Glasnost' (transparency). He also promoted the 'Paper of the Earth'; a document transmitted around the world about the need to look into and address the 'environmental emergency' and so ensure a future for our children.

Michael, the Archangel, takes us into a peaceful revolution of the soul, in which the coming of new humanity and of the 'New Earth' is prepared. The Planet is a spiritually evolved entity and speaks to its people to remind them, even in a traumatic way, that it needs to find an inner balance and a new harmony with the Universe. The world's greatest most significant changes are taking place on an energetic level. Ever more people want to learn new, natural techniques of relaxation, meditation and healing. There will be great changes in the way we think and see our future. We are part of a new reality that is evolving in an extraordinary way. Archangel Michael talks with passion to many 'channellers' today. These are people who feel the new Earth coming and their responsibility to bring information through. They task themselves to helping people to open up; to see beyond fears and limitations, to fly, to heal and to fight in the awareness of the spirit. He also talks through the thoughts of others, inspiring the people who feel him, like me, who are able to go forth and share his teachings.

For a long time now I have received messages from Archangel Michael. In the beginning these experiences have been quite difficult for me to accept; I did not feel prepared to accept that I had been one of the many people chosen for such channelling. Nowadays I feel more open to receive messages, even if when I talk about them in my seminars and lectures all over the world, people still roll their eyes, it is only when I start to talk to them about their problems or worries that they start believing. I strongly believe all of us are open to receive the voice of the Angels, we really just need to listen with an open heart. The fact that this has happened to me does not mean that I am a special person. I have just been chosen to be a channel at present for the people who care to listen to what I say in the simple way I am used to talking about spirituality. What has allowed me to become a clear channel of energy is the fact that I have been studying, practising and teaching Reiki/Universal Energy for many years now. Initially I did not realize how great this path I had chosen was, until now as I realize that Archangel Michael was there for me, working side by side to show me and teach me.

All that you find written here, I have received as inspiration from Archangel Michael and from those who have approached me as the 'Angels of Transparency' showing me the way forward. Michael is leading this group of 'new' Angels; they are all working together for the spiritual evolution of humankind. They have given me meditations and symbols that are 'prayers in action' and guide me through my work of opening hearts. These are the meditations and the symbols that I teach during my seminars as a new way that has been given to my heart. I feel a strong compulsion to give and receive energy, that is why I listen with my heart wide open and deliver the message. Michael pushes me to show courage, compassion and forgiveness to get to the core of the matter, to be free and finally released by all. That is why, together with Reiki and new forms of meditation and natural methods, I like going into nature and sacred places filled with the energy of Michael and feeling his presence there.

The presence of the Angels of Transparency is, for me, without a doubt, a reality that cannot be considered with science or objectivity, that belongs only to the material world. They should be measured with the inner truth that joins us to the spiritual world and has got its own way of manifesting. Scientific understanding talks about matter that can be measured but it is also starting to say something about energy, that it is the other aspect of matter; it is the part that gives matter a metaphysical or spiritual dimension. This energy cannot be calculated, but we can experience it. 'Spirit' is what you feel; it is the quality of our being. We are each responsible for our own 'energy' and custodian of it. We can share what we feel in our inner-self and what we receive as a gift from Spirit.

Part One of this book begins with a message from a spiritual source named 'Chung Fu', through Sally Pullinger (one of the greatest Trance Mediums I have found on my path). Chung Fu (which means 'inner truth') is described as a student of the ancient Chinese philosopher Lao Tzu, who taught that humans have immortal spirits that live through many incarnations until the individual identifies with a God-self during a life on Earth. These messages have confirmed my own guidance from the Angels of Transparency. Part one then continues with channelled messages from the Angels of Transparency. I act merely as the spokesperson and I try to keep as close as to the spoken version that was given as possible. In the other dimension we are all aware that time does not exist, because of that I have not recorded any dates and in some specific cases as I did not think it was necessary anyway. There are also meditations to accompany the Angels' words and a few supportive testimonials from my students, whom I thank.

Part Two of this book explains a little more of my 'path', what shaped me and lead me to my experiences with Reiki/Universal Energy and meditation. I also share with you what the encounters with the Archangels means to me, my practice and my development of Reiki and its relevance to our well-being today and further study cases. All these are the little steps I am taking to evolve and elevate my spirit and if these steps can help to ease your path in any way then all the better.

Part One

Messages
&
Meditations

CHAPTER I

EVOLUTION - CHUNG FU SPEAKS

At this time, many aspects of this life will change and recognize that there is a complete renewal about to transpire. From places where pollution has accumulated, there will be a great expulsion. Earth itself has the power to do this via earthquakes, volcanic eruptions, tidal waves and all manner of abnormal and unusual weather conditions. As these anomalies increase the planet itself starts shaking loose the shackles that have come to smother it over the last 500 years as humankind has ignored the profound and increasingly urgent warnings that emanate from the centre of the Earth. The Earth has accumulated a lot of debris that now must be discharged in order that 'Mother Nature', the metaphysical form of the planet itself, will continue to exist, flourish and evolve.

The destiny of our Earth is to continue to provide for human beings; for the very souls of human beings, the opportunity to grow, to understand and experience the third dimensional universe. However within that opportunity there is a contract, an agreement created by the star seed races who are about to return to re-establish this contract. Meanwhile some of the races who were permitted to come here in the interim will no longer be allowed to continue here and so there will be a noticeable change in the quality of human beings coming forward through the younger generations.

I speak about those who will arrive during the next 30 to 50 years and who will lead the collective consciousness into a new level of understanding. Of course that means there need to be places who will receive these very sensitive beings coming with a consciousness of an altogether different order. The need for the creation of such places of healing, of education, of sensitive guidance, is becoming more and more apparent in our culture. Forces or energies such as those that exist on the metaphysical plane are now encouraging many people to study subjects related to the above.

It will not be an easy undertaking to study the hearts and souls of humanity. In effect a 'spiritual' science. Ancient cultures always understood this as the highest science, and now this science will return in its true place within the cultures of humanity. Be not afraid to take this path that will be offered to you, for all around it has become possible once again through angelic intervention, enabling you to hear and see the manifestation of spirit as the astrophysical plane becomes visible to those eyes that are prepared for the vision.

Try to understand, during these times, that many challenges will be brought before you, but alongside these challenges of your inner-self like challenges of the heart, of the mind a vast energy, a force of spiritual will be present growing over the next fifty years. Alongside these angelic presences there will be also extraterrestrial presences of a benign nature coming in to balance certain energies of another order that has been present for the last few hundred years and has caused a certain amount of confusion and damage.

It was necessary to wait until now, until the veils were thinner, until people were able to feel the uncertainty and start finding within themselves a willingness to listen in order to seek an alternative to the chaos, the madness and the despair. That time has come. It is not only on Earth that there are beings who live in the physical dimension. There are many degrees of physicality in other star systems. Bodies may look different, but it is possible for those beings to travel 'astrally' to bring their consciousness to you and it is possible and it is happening more and more that beings are being assisted to connect with other galaxies, with other seed races who are preparing to come here.

Within your world the political systems are the most interesting elements for the beings who are travelling here from other places and who do not understand why it is that things have gone so wrong. What they find is that over the last few thousand years, the unity that was initially seeded here, has gone, and within the hearts of people, mistrust and suspicion has led to separation which is now at a peak within of all of the cultures, apart from, perhaps, some very ancient ones that still exist in hidden places in the world.

The beings who are born now, some of whom are coming into humanity from other star races, we will be able to rise high within the social political order that will bring about change that seems obvious to people once it is initiated but that presently has been blocked by the fear of the controlling powers in the world which are now starting to decline in number. What this means, is that deep within you it is possible to access of all which I speak through methods of inner exploration and 'journeying', and it is this latter method that needs to be studied now. It will lead to the opening of communication systems between the galaxies, between the present time people and the people who are arriving to take you into a new dimension.

The changes that are ahead of you will be of a physical nature on the Earth too. There will be the invasion in the coastal area of water that will rise and cause some damage. Some of these waters will flow in land in places where the land is low; the waters will overflow the banks of rivers. There will be some earth movement; it will not all happen at once, there will not be some great catastrophe where everything suddenly turns inside out. But in most places life will appear to go on much as normal, the change that will occur is within. You will find that somehow you are deeply affected by many things that are happening elsewhere. The terrible consequences of unexpected disasters will impact millions who witness these and are helpless to do anything about it.

A great sense of heartfelt compassion will come about from sharing in the emotional impacts of these disasters. Do not be afraid, the truth is that these events are occurring to enable a greater sense of enlightenment. Understand that as you journey through the next 10 to 30 years, the most important requirement for everyone is to simply become aware of the feelings within, to be in touch with the earth that is beneath your feet, to be more humble and grateful for the simple things in life like food and love, companionship and unity, harmony of mind, heart and body. These things, in truth, have been lost in modern times. They are the elements of grace that are returning despite what may appear to be disaster and catastrophe.

The Angels of Transparency have a strong connection with the Akashic Records *(coming from the Sanskrit word 'akasha', meaning, 'sky', 'space', 'ether', and is said to be an account of all things that have been, are and will come to pass, held in another dimension, also known as 'Book of life' and 'Memory of Nature)'* and the Crystal Beings, whom I also refer to as Angels. There is a lot of energy passing between the two. The Angels of Transparency, I also refer to as the Guardians, because they are the holders of the heart. People need a lot of courage to find the truth within themselves. The Guardians deal with the wounds of the heart and often it is some knowledge or memory that is trapped in the heart that the Guardians and Crystal beings can unlock by accessing the Akashic Records, making sense of and 'exorcising' the memory which then free it from the heart. Without this release and deeper understanding that comes from the connection to the Akashic Records you would be unable to fully partake of this life.

There is a real concentration at this present time because of the call to human consciousness to open up the heart centre and once again find the value of simplicity, of presence, of love, of everything that I have mentioned. Because of that, these Angelic Realms are coming closer and closer. For the last hundred years and the last 50 years in particular, it has been very difficult to connect with the Angelic Realm, now gateways are opening again and it has been possible for these beings to come very, very close to the hearts and minds of people again.

CHAPTER 2

THE ANGELS SPEAK

It is very important to pray for others, because when you pray for someone, an angel goes and sits on the shoulder of that person.
THE VIRGIN MARY, TO THE CHILDREN AT
MEDJUGORIE

The Angels of Transparency are led by Archangel Metatron and Archangel Michael. Metatron is a great Angel who helps us to understand ourselves better. He is often depicted surrounded by a purple/red light, astride a wagon. Michael is the Archangel who defeats evil. He is always depicted with a sword and long blond hair. In religious iconography he is shown with the devil at his feet. In energetic treatments and in Reiki we always call upon him to free us from temptation and fear. The Angels of Transparency are here now and are advising me that the time has finally come to speak.

Today is January 27th, 2006. It is an important date. In terms of numerology, it is number '9' and nine symbolizes an ending. So this leads to another 'beginning'; the beginning of this work. The Angels of Transparency are here and they are showing me two Earths. The Earth of the third dimension; where we live now and have destroyed through war, greed and chemistry and an Earth of the fifth dimension, that has already been prepared for this next transition.

The Creatures of Light (Lightworkers) are helping those who still live in darkness to make this transition. This transition will end around 2012, when all of us will be more aware, when all will have gained 'higher consciousness,' recognized across religious, spiritual and metaphysical establishments and has recently been commonly referred to as 'Super Consciousness' or 'Christ Consciousness' as coined by the New Thought Movement in the late 19th century. The year 2012 will not be the end of the world, as an entity in itself, but it will be the end of this 'older' version, which is now so gripped by conflict and misunderstanding. In order to get there we need to be ready; to prepare for the light.

The Angels of Transparency show me this world as though it were split in two, like two halves of an orange. On one side, there are the Lightworkers, those who live in the light and who are aware of the energy and vibrational treatments. Without doubt they are fewer in number than those who live on the other side in darkness. It is as though small lights are turning on in some people in this group, and these people, little by little, are lighting up and moving to the other side. The lights are their hearts sparking into life. These hearts are lighting up a little at a time, so the people are lighting up too.

Very soon, the people who choose not to light up will be leaving this Earth. The people who are alight will evolve. When we say that people are 'alight', we are talking about those who have opened their hearts to this feeling, to this fluidity, to this energy. People who will have been thus 'illuminated' will regain internal peace, serenity, internal joy, communion and brotherhood. They will regain a harmony that will be important for future Earth. Earth is changing quickly and it is vital that we all feel 'as One' in unity with God.

The Angels of Transparency are telling me that the time has come for people to be 'transparent'; to be honest with themselves and with each other, to be open, to open their hearts, the chakras of the heart, to reveal their innocence, to show their vulnerability, to demonstrate their ability to love and to love unconditionally. And when the Angels of Transparency are around us, we feel warmth in the chakra of the third eye and an intense glow in the heart chakra. It is the heart chakra that enables us to open our hearts by 360 degrees and for our hearts to beat not only for us and for our loved ones, but for those whom we do not know as well. It is important for us to create this new 'Earth of the Fifth Dimension', so that it may contain only peace, love, harmony and brotherhood.

To be 'transparent' is to be open and available. This state of 'availability' is what prepares the new world of peace and harmony. We should be open, having the courage to be vulnerable at times, we need to be at peace with ourselves; we need to always try to make peace with those we have fought. We should forgive, as forgiveness is very important. We can evolve spiritually only by forgiving. We should never be resentful or hate other people. To forgive oneself and others is important in order to evolve spiritually.

The 'Energy of Transformation' has very little weight, but it is strong. When it touches us, we can feel a whirling wind coming from the first chakra, a whirlwind of light, of fresh energy that originates from the first chakra and develops upwards. This is the physical manifestation of the Energy of Transformation. It originates from a superior strength; from the Angels of Transparency. These Angels have not appeared before many people; but there are other channels in the world who are all receiving the same information. These people are not familiar with each other, and I do not know about the other people. Nevertheless, at a certain point in time, there will be books leading to a single explanation; and these books will be published around the world.

The Angels of Transparency are young Angels, connected with an ancient lost continent in the Pacific Ocean, that pre-dates Atlantis, referred to as the 'Motherland' or 'Mu' and in more modern times linked to the popular, mythical, Lemuria. It is believed that the civilization of this land has long been lost, but there is a belief that it still exists, is highly evolved and acts as a channel for us to receive healing, techniques for transformation and spiritual evolution. The Angels of Transparency are also connected to the star cluster of Pleiades.

Earth is changing. Its inhabitants are experiencing spiritual evolution. It is very important to listen; people can hear, but they do not listen. Listen with the heart. If someone is speaking - telling a story - listen to them. These are years of total transformation, they are miraculous years. Everything that is requested will be granted in accordance with the Divine Light. The Angels will give the world strong and powerful meditations, leading to peace, tranquility and harmony in our hearts. For this to happen their hearts must be completely open.

Luminous Earth Meditation

Sit or lay down comfortably. Close your eyes and pay attention to your senses. Breathe deeply. Consciously inhale and exhale. Fill your lungs completely with air; feel the air go into your lungs and come out through your mouth and nose. Each time you breathe, feel yourself become more relaxed. Inhale, pulling in to your breath, your inner energies, experience their colours and feel their warmth. Hold your breath for a few seconds, and as you exhale feel all the unwanted energy and any blockages leave your body. Keep breathing deeply.

Listen to your breath. Using your 'inner' vision see your tummy rise and fall and scan every part of your body; seeing each organ, muscle, nerve, every fibre of your physical being become relaxed. Keep breathing deeply and relax further.

Imagine your body surrounded by rings of coloured, warm light. Pay attention to your eyelids, the little muscles around your eyes and let them go. Relax your forehead and cheeks. Keep breathing deeply and steadily. Relax your lips, leave your mouth ajar. Relax your neck and shoulders by massaging them with your imagination. Caress your neck and gently flex it, allowing the shoulders to drop and relax. Your neck and shoulders are given respite from supporting the head, letting go of all tension. Slowly continue to relax every part of your body. Keep breathing deeply, remaining mindful of your breathing and keeping your eyes closed.

Visualize that you are weightless and suspended in space. From where you are, look at planet Earth. It is your planet, your home and it is suspended in the space, just like you are. It is blue and green, just beautiful. It is where you live, where universal love has taken you to enjoy yourself in human form and from where you will return to the infinite. Your eyes are filled with love and gratitude for the Earth that supports you in this journey. Feel your bond with Earth and how it makes you capable of opening up to the light.

In the core of the Earth a little flame of universal energy is set alight. A flame of Universal healing energy which is the same one we have in the centre of our own hearts. As this expands in ourselves so the little flame becomes a fire of healing exuding from the centre of the Earth. It is a fire that does not burn, rather it is a fire of energy and love that, as it expands heals all the people of the Earth and all the minds of those above us. Gradually this flame envelops the entire Earth and the hearts and minds of the people are purified, healed, refreshed and the Earth begins to heal. Forests, air and seas are cleared and humankind begins to feel like nature is a part of their life. A need to protect animals and plants is born. Humankind becomes respectful and thankful of the living energy that gives it life on earth.

The Earth is now simmering with energy and comes slowly out of the chaos. It finds harmony, as we find harmony inside ourselves. With all the other people whose hearts are now open, look at the Earth illuminated from within and from without, transparent and beautiful. Thank her for all she gives us. Reassure and tell her that you will keep feeling this bond of which you are now conscious and this gratitude towards her. See how your heart is now wide open and how Earth has begun to flourish and give you peace and everything you need. Keep gazing upon hugging the Earth.

Now, slowly return to this space. Breathe deeply. Remain, few more minutes with your eyes closed. Feel your body and your breath. Gradually come back and open your eyes, feeling tranquil and serene; harmonious and with a profound sense of gratitude and love. Listen to your senses and notice how the contact with the Earth has transformed you and has opened you to unknown realities and dimensions. Feel how much you are ready now to heal your internal battles, to be in balance and in harmony, now you are supported by the strength of the Earth as she has been supported by your Love and from the profound love of all the people like yourself.

CHAPTER 3

OVERCOMING OBSTACLES

The greatest obstacles to an open heart are politics, power, and the pursuit of dirty money; money that is not earned honestly. People need to open their minds and hearts to the idea that money is only energy and therefore it must be respected and used. It is of no use to ask for money and material aid in our prayers. We need to look deep into our hearts, in order to receive the energy of prosperity, which should be used for humanitarian rather than materialistic ends.

On this Earth there are many people who are already more spiritually evolved than most. It is believed they came to us in the main during the 1960s onwards, though a few will have been born before. They are popularly referred to as 'indigo children'. Indigo children are seen as people gifted with superior energies and are here on Earth to help our spiritual evolution. Earth will witness a convergence of planets that will cause the energy of these people to propel us forward and great discoveries will follow as part of a sudden spiritual evolution. For example we will be able to 'see' what ails us as our bodies adopt an ability to become transparent. Telepathy will allow people to love unconditionally. It will be possible to receive answers telepathically.

Right now though, there are power structures that conceal these messages from the Angels. But soon the planets will converge, the 'indigo children' will become outraged and there will be a series of catastrophic events. People will simply 'disappear' to make way for more evolved spirits to arrive. Lightworkers are making space for these 'pure energy channels'. Some are already here, ready to help. A shining spirit of cooperation will emerge. Especially among all those who assist in opening hearts and helping children.

Today the word 'transparency' is used in many messages, in many advertisements and in many broadcasts. This is because these Angels are trying to make the world more transparent – honest. Those who want to understand will understand. This is what the Angels of Transparency are telling me now, "We, the Angels of Transparency are here today so that you may understand, deep in your hearts, what transparency is. Transparency is honesty. Transparency is linearity and simplicity. Transparency means having a good heart, being kind. It will also be necessary to study and understand what happens after death and prior to birth. There are many people who already know about life beyond death. Life beyond life, the tunnel we all need to pass through, the Akashic Library, where all the names and memories of all the people who have lived on Earth in any place and at any time are kept. This great library also preserves the secret of birth and coming on Earth. To understand it will be a huge step forward as it will make it possible for people to dispel the fear of death and to be open to transformation.

Another obstacle to be overcome in this time of transformation is fatigue. You feel tired and at times you are confused because passing from one Earth to the other is a very intense experience that leaves you completely exhausted. But you need to take this step now because, in point of fact, you are helping others open their hearts, awaken their souls, their minds, their spirits and their bodies. By doing this, passing from one Earth to the other, you are helping more people even more: evolution is getting faster and faster all the time. But you must all be ready to face a new reality, so even if you happen to feel tired, exhausted, and without energy, you must know that, with the instructions that we will give you, you will be able to achieve added peace, greater love, and a more serene frame of mind to help all those who will reach out to you.

The Angels of Transparency have gifted me a wonderful

meditation with the Archangel Raphael, the Archangel of Healing. It is called the 'Healing Breath'. It is a very strong and powerful meditation and it is appropriate when clusters of negative energy have formed. Thanks to the Archangel's breath, these clusters, or energy dust, will go away. The breath gets rid of all the energies a person no longer needs.

Healing Breath Meditation

Sit or lay down comfortably. Close your eyes and pay attention to your senses. Breathe deeply. Consciously inhale and exhale. Fill your lungs completely with air; feel the air go into your lungs and come out through your mouth and nose. Each time you breathe, feel yourself become more relaxed. Inhale, pulling in to your breath, your inner energies, experience their colours and feel their warmth. Hold your breath for a few seconds, and as you exhale feel all the unwanted energy and any blockages leave your body. Keep breathing deeply.

Listen to your breath. Using your 'inner' vision see your tummy rise and fall and scan every part of your body; seeing each organ, muscle, nerve, every fibre of your physical being become relaxed. Keep breathing deeply and relax further.

Imagine your body surrounded by rings of coloured, warm light. Pay attention to your eyelids, the little muscles around your eyes and let them go. Relax your forehead and cheeks. Keep breathing deeply and steadily. Relax your lips, leave your mouth ajar. Relax your neck and shoulders by massaging them with your imagination. Caress your neck and gently flex it, allowing the shoulders to drop and relax. Your neck and shoulders are given respite from supporting the head, letting go of all tension. Slowly continue to relax every part of your body. Keep breathing deeply, remaining mindful of your breathing and keeping your eyes closed.

Now just above you visualize Archangel Raphael, the Healing Archangel. Look at him. You can see his emerald green healing ray enter your crown chakra with a gentle blow. Keep breathing slowly and steadily as you feel his green energy entering your body, clearing all negativity around and inside you. Feel his green energy pervading your body and your organs, purifying and cleansing all unwanted thoughts from your inner body like a breeze blowing through you. Keep breathing deeply and steadily.

Archangel Raphael helps people who are suffering with his

divine breath; his breath is healing. He is upon you and continues to blow in healing energy to clear and heal you. It is like a fresh and clean wind.

With each intake of breath, feel the energy moving through you restoring and recharging you with strength and confidence. Raphael is with you to remind you that your life is in your hands and you can make room for your best energies with his help. With each out breath, rid yourself of dirt, dust and density, which vanishes into thin air and disappears forever.

Inhale and feel the green energy coming inside you. Exhale, letting go of everything that you do not need in the body anymore. Breathe in the energy and then expel the waste. Inhale. Exhale.

Now ask Raphael to support and assist you with his energy. Ask him to guide and protect you in this process. Feel his powerful and nurturing energy continue to fill you with healing and positivity. Remember to ask for his guidance every day of your life and whenever you need it. Raphael is here for you to heal all fears, remove any indecision and tension. His breath continues to support and clear you.

Again inhale and feel the green energy coming inside you. Exhale, letting go of everything that you do not need in the body anymore. Breathe in the energy and then expel the waste. Inhale. Exhale.

Now slowly come back into this space and into the place in which you are resting. Keep breathing deeply and steadily. Keep your eyes closed and feel your body and your breath. Slowly now, come back, open your eyes and you will feel a sense of peace, serenity and harmony around you. Breathe slowly and sense how Raphael's green ray of light has completely cleared and purified and energized you from within.

CHAPTER 4

NATURAL HARMONY

The new Earth in the Fifth Dimension is ready to welcome its children. It is very important for us to know that it is there, ready to welcome us all. Certainly, not everyone will be ready for this spiritual journey and many will leave their bodies not being able to survive the huge transformation that this Earth is undergoing. But most people will be able to see and live in the New Earth, provided that people learn to harmonize with Nature; the daughter of the meeting of our Heaven and Earth. We are Nature.

We can recover this conscience; an awareness that has been lost by giving over to the false belief that we are something different from the Natural World. We can do it by meditating on Nature and in Nature. We owe our very existence to the Natural World. Do this by meditating on trees, animals and the beauty of creation. Imagine that your body is like a tree. When you are born it is like a small shoot that grows and develops into a tree; your arms and legs are the branches of this tree, your feet are the roots, your nose and your mouth are the leaves that nourish you and your internal organs are like the chlorophyll inside the tree. This is a simple, yet powerful meditation that makes you feel at one with Nature and with the New Earth that is emerging and coming to life.

Go out into Nature and feel its life-giving flow. Let it run through you as rain or river water flowing everywhere, without ever asking for anything in return and all the while quenching the thirst of everyone and everything, then flowing out to the sea, only to return to the sky and fall back to Earth once again. This is how water binds us to the entire Universe that lives within us. Now feel the love the nourishment creates and note your heart becomes love. That love is everywhere, in every living thing and in every object that exists. You will soon be returning to the genuine and natural things that can open your heart.

Once you are ready to open your heart, that you are capable of understanding your evolving nature, you will find it easier to contemplate Nature itself. Only a small percentage of the people who live on Earth today are capable of being truly 'aware' of the Natural World, of the songs of the birds and of the sounds of the sea, and able to truly admire Nature's beauty. But a day will come when all on Earth will be able to contemplate silence and love and be capable of loving unconditionally. Many before the Angels of Transparency have tried this, but the time has now come for a massive spiritual evolution that will transform all of Earth's inhabitants. I am told that we are on the right track.

Meditate on animals, who are our brothers and sisters, and who, just like people, have a conscience and sensitivity and are also evolving. The Angels stress two important connections that we should try to make with the Animal Kingdom; one being to swim with the dolphins in the ocean. Another is to go whale watching. These 'beings of light' are extremely important for Earth's evolution. The origin of all marine mammals is the land. These mammals evolved, choosing to make their home in the sea. We should look upon them as the *Angels of the Sea*, who will speak to us and die for us. Dolphins are closely connected to us, telepathically. They have a chakra of the third eye that is very open and developed and they have a chakra of the heart that is also fully open. Their chakras are different from ours as they obviously do not have a fifth chakra of the throat separate from the chakra of the heart. In dolphins, these two chakras are one: this is how their wonderful love songs are born. They have sensory chakras that assist in their own evolution and in the evolution of humanity. It is important for everyone to understand the importance of these beings.

Metatron, the Lord Metatron, who appears on a wagon, is

also the Archangel of the Sea and many of the Lightworkers who live on the planet today are aware of the vibrations that the sea gives us. They are conscious of the tremendous importance of the sea and its inhabitants. It is important for us to listen to the sounds of the sea, to listen to the songs of whales and dolphins. These sounds help our hearts to evolve.

But all animals, not just the ones that live in the sea, were created to assist in human evolution. They too, are following their own evolution, and have become accustomed to mankind. At this time we are only able to say that elephants are just as evolved as whales and that the 'dancing' (a term used to describe ritual movements the animals par-take in at certain times of the year) of elephants and whales, makes it possible for the energetic axis of planet Earth to be balanced, in harmony with these dances and in harmony with the heart chakra of the Earth, thus, with the heart chakras of people.

However, it is important to assist in the evolution of the animals inhabiting the Earth today. This way we also will help ourselves. Help those, who persecute these animals, to better understand and open their hearts. With the help of the many new spirits, which are now being created for the New Earth, it will be a land of peace, brotherhood and harmony.

The Natural World is our home, our mother and our life. People need to go back to Nature, to embracing trees. Visualize the chlorophyll in trees, as though in our bodies; the sap of trees is as vital as the lymph in our bodies. What can possibly bring greater joy to our hearts than listening to the chirping of birds, out in the open, or smelling the perfume of flowers?

Nature protects us while we open up to the transparency of the heart. It protects us by making us a gift of the mediations on the natural elements: water, earth, fire, and air. And it is important for people to meditate on easy, natural things, to be able to relax, become confident, well-balanced and healed. We mustn't deal with difficult subjects or pursue complicated meditations: the power of nature will heal us, in its simplicity.

Water cleans and refreshes you, it nourishes you. It is transparent, it goes everywhere and it gives you all the energy you need. It refreshes and heartens you. Meditating on fire is a way to warm your soul and your heart, if they have grown cold for some reason. Meditating on air is focusing awareness on breath, on the wind. Wind is a source of lightness, freshness, and freedom. Meditation on Earth is about sap and trees.

When you don't feel 'grounded', as if you are losing your grasp on reality, like you are suspended in thin air without any control over what is happening to you, seek out a place of natural healing, like a garden or a park and walk barefoot amongst the plants and wildlife. This process will allow you to regain contact or a physical connection with Earth and Nature. It will give you a sense of being 'rooted' in this world again.

Lay down in a field of green grass and listen only to the sounds of Nature; the rustling of leaves in the wind, the calls of animals, the sounds of insects around you, the chirping of birds, the beating of their wings. Quite simply, experience the feeling of the earth, the grass, the lawn and the roots in the ground. Imagine roots sprouting from the chakras in your feet and holding you completely to the ground, until you feel as one with planet Earth.

The Angels of Transparency tell me that it is absolutely essential that people live on Earth more naturally. This is how it will be in the future. People who will be successful in opening their hearts will have a successful voyage. The Angels define this group of people as those who will become aware of their soul, their spirit, and their body.

In the New Earth, there will be an increasing use of crystals, multi-coloured crystals. Crystals are the transparency of Nature, the joining of light and matter and the Angels of Transparency tell me that we are the same. Crystals heal because they remind us of this fact and thereby purify us. They take away our anxiety by rebalancing the energy that is always flowing between spirit and matter. When we lose sight of the importance of this equilibrium, we run the real danger of becoming trapped in our minds which makes us identify either only with spirit or only with matter.

But Nature binds the two, and Nature's crystals are exactly this: Nature in which pure light is expressed. Crystals remind you that you are one and the other combined, in balance, that spirit and matter are two sides of the same coin. They hearten and allow one to see things as they are, clearly. They will allow you to see matter, and then beyond matter, to see the spirit and then beyond spirit.

The Angels of Transparency gift with us a wonderful meditation that now follows which helps to ground and rebalance us, connecting us to all creation, allowing us to feel truly alive and in harmony with all.

Tree Of Light Meditation

Sit or lay down comfortably. Close your eyes and pay attention to your senses. Breathe deeply. Consciously inhale and exhale. Fill your lungs completely with air; feel the air go into your lungs and come out through your mouth and nose. Each time you breathe, feel yourself become more relaxed. Inhale, pulling in to your breath, your inner energies, experience their colours and feel their warmth. Hold your breath for a few seconds, and as you exhale feel all the unwanted energy and any blockages leave your body. Keep breathing deeply.

Listen to your breath. Using your 'inner' vision see your tummy rise and fall and scan every part of your body; seeing each organ, muscle, nerve, every fibre of your physical being become relaxed. Keep breathing deeply and relax further.

Imagine your body surrounded by rings of coloured, warm light. Pay attention to your eyelids, the little muscles around your eyes and let them go. Relax your forehead and cheeks. Keep breathing deeply and steadily. Relax your lips, leave your mouth ajar. Relax your neck and shoulders by massaging them with your imagination. Caress your neck and gently flex it, allowing the shoulders to drop and relax. Your neck and shoulders are given respite from supporting the head, letting go of all tension. Slowly continue to relax every part of your body. Keep breathing deeply, remaining mindful of your breathing and keeping your eyes closed.

Now imagine being a seed in the ground. Feel the land around you; its warmth and protection. Sense the water in the land as it travels through bringing vitality and nourishment. There is a desire within you to germinate and grow, to live and expand. Feel the water feeding you salts and nutrients. You are a seed that grows, expands and opens. Small roots sprout from your feet going deeper into the ground. Feel like they are exploring and advancing in the land in search of balance.

Now the little bud is growing slowly and steadily towards

the sky. Keep breathing and absorbing the vital force. Hear the calling from above; life that expands with every breath you take. The little bud is growing and now there is a small leaf coming out of it…

Slowly unfold your legs and arms and stand up finding your balance on your feet, with your legs slightly bent. You are that little bud that comes out of the ground and goes toward the sky. Slowly stretch your legs and arms towards the sky. Tilt your head up and keep stretching

Now notice how you expand into the earth as roots sprout from your feet. Feel how your feet sink into the earth in search of water and nutrients. Notice the way in which the earth feeds you; through your roots, your feet into your legs and up through your torso. Your torso is the trunk of the tree, and through it the earth is feeding the branches that are represented by your outstretched arms. From branches sprout buds and leaves.

Feel how your lips, your nose, your ears, your skin have become leaves and receive all information; sounds smells and light of the world. Feel how your leaves open and fly into the air. Experience the feeling of each leaf as, one by one they unfold widen and relax, open to receive the light. Listen how they absorb the light while swaying in the wind. The air gently caresses the leaves that absorb light and enjoy the heat.

Experience what it feels like inside the leaves where the magic of photosynthesis occurs; as the light manifests into its physical essence and it becomes sweet nutrients that help you to grow, becoming strong and beautiful. With every breath you take, feel this pure nourishment feed the life force within you. Keep breathing slowly and deeply.

And now you can feel the light meshing with every part of you, becoming part of your body allowing you to be part of this world.

Now listen as flowers emerge from the branches; blossoming everywhere. Now that you're in the light it fills you with vigour and the desire to open and extend your life force. You desire to give love and spread life and beauty everywhere. Feel your flowers opening their petals to the sun. Listen to them swaying in the wind along with the branches and leaves. Keep breathing slowly and deeply.

Observe as the flowers become fruit. Small green fruit first, then increasingly larger and more mature. In the fruits there is a fullness; there are the seeds that you will again give to the world to restore life and the love of life which you have grown. Keep breathing deeply and slowly.

The fruits are now ready to open; becoming food for other life forms as they fall and start sowing their seeds. Experience again what it is like to be the seed, relying on the wind and the earth. The wind and the birds carrying some of the seeds away. The earth receives some of them, takes them with her and feeds them. Keep breathing deeply and slowly.

Listen to all that is happening around you; insects, birds, shrubs, rocks and grass. Feel how you continue to receive energy from the air, food and support from below. Feel how your life is at one with all nature around you. Feel the trees around you and imagine they are like your brothers who share the same life and the same light. Keep breathing deeply and slowly.

Now open your eyes. Slowly crouch down on the floor with the palms of your hands flat on the ground and let the energy from your palms run into the earth. Then feel the energy, the life force come back to you, entering into you through your palms. Slowly rise up and bring that energy above you up to your head and raising your hands release it into the sky. Now visualize this energy coming back down through you from above.

Relax your arms and stand still, breathing deeply and slowly for a few moments to finish the mediation.

CHAPTER 5

FORGIVE & GIVE IN

The most important thing on Earth, right now, is our ability to forgive. Forgiving others and above all, ourselves, for having been caught in situations that were, perhaps, not very happy. Then there are those around you, whom you hurt, perhaps without even knowing. There are people who have suffered abuse; physical, psychological and sexual. These are such incredibly traumatic experiences that seem impossible to forgive.

But it is very important for the people who have committed wrongdoings to be forgiven, so that especially those who have endured the abuse may be set free and break the karmic chain that ties a person to the situation. When the abused are unable to forgive, they remain chained to the event. To forgive is to express unconditional love. To 'for-give' is giving, it is love, it makes it possible to cleanse ourselves, to become independent, detached from the material sphere and to live solely in pure love.

The Angels of Transparency tell me that as Earth evolves, you will be able to detach yourself from the material sphere and live in energy, to be free, elevated, for the body and even the soul to feel lighter. For example, our shoulders energetically bear the weight of attachment to people and are permeated by the vibrations of these people. If you clean your auras and your chakras by forgiving people, letting them go, abandoning any resentment, you will find yourself once again in a state of lightness, fluidity, universal love, the pure energy of love. It is difficult, but it is possible and the only thing to do.

In the coming years there will be a huge spiritual awakening; a great opening. It will involve many, who will decide to put their heart into everything they do, without any doubt and without any hesitation. They won't need to ask questions because they will find the answers even before asking. To forgive and to give in, surrender. Let's see a white flag. A white flag means to surrender. To surrender is to cease fighting. Things will come of their own accord. These are the 'miracle years'. All you need to do is ask, but you need to ask simply and clearly. Just ask in the present and things will happen.

Surrendering is to 'give' in to the situation. Accept and embrace what life brings you. Find all that is good, in everything. Even in pain and suffering, as these are the steps of transformation. The Angels tell me that we are infinite beings who simply go through this life on our greater journey. Those who suffer will find help; those who can help will find a way. We will be able to carry the light. But we will need to let go, with forgiveness and surrendering our negative energies, even if we have suffered. And those who have suffered may in turn help those who are still suffering and this will give meaning to their suffering and it will open his or her heart and the hearts of others.

I have spoken generally about forgiving and surrendering and with the permission of two of my Reiki students I would like to share their stories now as examples of how this principle applies to our lives now. The first relates to a man from Milan who at 26 years old has a very responsible job within the fashion industry. He had never been involved with Reiki or anything like it. We met by accident, in a hotel where he was staying with his father. When he heard that I was a Reiki master, and his own father taking an interest, he reacted badly. He accused his father of doubting God, of being involved in the Occult and taking part in fraudulent activities. He is a practicing Catholic, attending both church services and church activities and he had heard bad things about Reiki. He witnessed large numbers of people coming to me for a consultation, and it all seemed absurd to him. He had an excellent relationship with his father, so it was painful for him to see his father interested in what, in his eyes, was something phony.

When he found out that I was going to hold an entry-level Reiki class in Milan, he thought, 'Why not?' His need to explore the unknown made him fast to act. He came to the class without expectations, but with an open mind. He was baffled by people who cried immediately, or were overwhelmed, and his girlfriend was among these. His father was there too. During the meditations, others could see things from their past, but he couldn't see anything and he admitted it openly.

But then he too felt something, which he now calls a moment of 'high spirituality', a sense of 'brotherhood' and this triggered a recollection. He remembered when, as a child, he went to the mountains with his church group. He was in a field and he could smell the grass and had that same sensation of freedom and innocence. And suddenly he remembered something else: a friend of his who had died in a motorbike accident. They had been friends for fifteen years, and yet, when he heard of his death, he almost failed to react. He was far away from Milan and he didn't feel the slightest desire either to mourn his friend or go to the funeral. Then, at that moment during the class, he felt sad. His girlfriend sensed something and asked him what was wrong. It was then that he started to cry. It had been ten years since he had cried. He was desperate.

In the meantime, I had finished with that part of the class and asked him to stay a while longer. He wanted to go home, he was frightened. I asked him what had happened and told him that he was not crying for his friend, but that the Angels had chosen his friend to push the barriers that he had built up. He cried for an hour, but he kept saying, 'Look, there is no barrier to remove.' I told him that there was someone he had to forgive.

He spoke of his father and a time when he was about five years old. His father was not well, and would come home drunk and verbally abuse his mother. This behaviour had lasted for only a short period of time before everything had gone back to normal, but he had cut off his feelings towards his father since then. It was a deep sorrow that had hurt him and that he had forgotten about. He had built barriers around this incident and no longer realized that he had. I told him that the barriers were so tall that it would actually take very little effort to bring them down. The strange thing is that he had confronted the issue at a rational level and had even spoken to his father about it. But I told him that he had stopped crying since then because he was too busy 'running'.

At that point he told me he was feeling very strong contractions, almost as though something else was being dislodged. I told him that he had someone else to forgive. It took him many long minutes to understand, but he then realized that it was him! He had never forgiven himself. He was the 'evil one'. He let others go if they could not keep up with him. He had become cold, isolated. For something basically quite small he had changed his nature, he had abandoned that child. He thought that he was cold and aloof, but it was a cover. Then I told him to remember when he was a child, alone in bed crying. He said he could see himself there, it really felt like he was in his room, he could even see his short pants with patches and he could smell himself as a child. And then he hugged himself, as one hugs a child. He said that these were times that he could recall, but as if through a veil; now he felt sorry for that child that he had so long chosen to deny.

All this happened at the beginning of the Reiki class. Although this lasted only fifteen minutes, he realized that it had changed his life. Had he gone to a psychoanalyst it would have taken years to make this discovery. His father was attending the class too and understanding what had happened, he could not speak to his son for three days. He had once again recognized the eyes of that child. My client realized that the question he had held back since then was, 'Dad, why are you making Mummy cry?' And he had been running away ever since. He also told me that the ongoing back pain and the pain in his side, which had been strong enough to make him cry at times and remain bedridden for days, were relieved through Reiki. When he feels any discomfort now he just does Reiki. He also realizes that there are other interesting and important things in life besides his faith.

My second account is about Giuseppe's journey. He and I met at a conference. It was a strange period in his life; Giuseppe is a nuclear engineer and teaches in a college. Many students approach him asking advice about life's problems rather than physics. He does his best to help. He noticed that he is able to help a lot of people with his words and compassion, often getting people through very dark periods in life. Many people are going through a transformation. They don't know what to do and how to approach the changes.

Giuseppe could relate to this general feeling of disorientation, he had felt this himself, years before. His mentor often says that we are surrounded by spiritual guides and Giuseppe has found many on his path. He feels his time with me and working with Reiki has allowed him to tangibly experience a new dimension, one where matter meets the spirit. It is the sphere in which we enter into relations with others. For Giuseppe it was already clear, intellectually, that we are always in relation with others, but now he can feel the soul, there is a certainty that allows him to express and live his life to the full. Now he knows that nothing happens by chance. Giuseppe said even the teachings and parables of Christ now seem very clear, everything 'rings a bell' as if he sees it with more clarity and simplicity.

During my lecture on Reiki, I simply put my hands on Giuseppe's head. He felt a sense of deep relaxation and comfort. It was quite an experience of spiritual opening. He has always prayed for people's healing, but with Reiki he was able to see it, even at a distance. Each time you give Reiki to someone the Universal Energy clears and cleans you first, as we must become a clear channel, in order to help others. Giuseppe told me he experiences Reiki as an energy that arrives as a stream at first, very soft, very intense. It is a sweet and warm current that is experienced as a sense of harmony that pervades us. When you feel this harmony, then you can channel pure love energy for others. Giuseppe says I have helped him to see and sense the Energy that allows him to first help himself and then to help others.

He talks of our relationship as that of two kindred spirits, like he has found his twin brother, like a relationship that already existed before we met. Giuseppe felt I was able to extract qualities in him that he was unaware of. At the end of the conference he queued for an hour to talk to me and was surprised when I told him that I had felt his soul; that he could give more to others. We stayed in touch and Giuseppe undertook Reiki training. Giuseppe realized after years of studying and learning Reiki that everybody has this gift inside. He concludes that, thanks to the Universal Energy, he can help others and be aware of the other dimensions and invisible beings around us. The best thing he discovered is that we can learn from pain. Pain is the last opportunity we have to learn, it is the consequence of karma, of past actions that we do not understand, and of those of past lives. That is why Reiki is a way to clear, help and give a sense to pain to evolve and transform our lives.

Now I end this chapter with a meditation that will enable you to immerse, and purify yourself. Cleanse and re-energize as you go through the process of forgiving and giving in to past hurts and blockages and releasing pre-conceived ideas and beliefs, seeing things differently, from a new perspective.

Pure Water Meditation

Sit or lay down comfortably. Close your eyes and pay attention to your senses. Breathe deeply. Consciously inhale and exhale. Fill your lungs completely with air; feel the air go into your lungs and come out through your mouth and nose. Each time you breathe, feel yourself become more relaxed. Inhale, pulling in to your breath, your inner energies, experience their colours and feel their warmth. Hold your breath for a few seconds, and as you exhale feel all the unwanted energy and any blockages leave your body. Keep breathing deeply.

Listen to your breath. Using your 'inner' vision see your tummy rise and fall and scan every part of your body; seeing each organ, muscle, nerve, every fibre of your physical being become relaxed. Keep breathing deeply and relax further.

Imagine your body surrounded by rings of coloured, warm light. Pay attention to your eyelids, the little muscles around your eyes and let them go. Relax your forehead and cheeks. Keep breathing deeply and steadily. Relax your lips, leave your mouth ajar. Relax your neck and shoulders by massaging them with your imagination. Caress your neck and gently flex it, allowing the shoulders to drop and relax. Your neck and shoulders are given respite from supporting the head, letting go of all tension. Slowly continue to relax every part of your body. Keep breathing deeply, remaining mindful of your breathing and keeping your eyes closed.

Now imagine Archangel Raphael. You can see his emerald green healing ray enter your crown chakra with a gentle blow. Breathe slowly and steadily as you feel his green energy pervading your body and your organs, purifying and cleansing all unwanted thoughts keep breathing deeply and steadily.

Now visualize your body as a crystal box; translucent and empty. Yours has a strong shell, you can feel the strength, but it has nothing inside. Prepare to allow your body to open welcome in the energy of the universe.

Now look at your body again and notice you can see your chakras emanating coloured energy. Visualize your chakras rotating like spirals or luminous flowers. They are the centre of your body, but their light, their colour and their vibration extend beyond body.

Next see yourself being immersed in clear, clean water. Your body floats without weight, but with grace and lightness. Let your body rest in the water floating and feeling the flow of water going around your body. Now you feel the pure water entre your crown chakra. Gradually the flow becomes stronger and more intense. See how the flow of the energy in the water it surrounds you and becomes one with you.

The clear water keeps flowing quietly. The water fills your body, talking on the colours of the chakras, washing, clearing and energizing your entire being. Feel the water coming from the universe to fill your entire body. The water enters from the crown chakras and fills your forehead. It fills your eyes nose and mouth and ears, it fills your neck and moves down through your shoulders, chest, arms and hand.

The water touches and is absorbed by all of your organs, your heart, lungs and kidneys and fills the intestine, cleaning and sweeping away all the energy you no longer need. The water continues to flow down through your hips and thighs, knees, calves, ankles and your feet.

The water continues to flow through you, to enter and leave you, giving you strength, energy and food and cleaning up all the energies you no longer need. This energy, this transparent clear and fresh water clears, cleans and regenerates you relieving all the stresses of the day.

Slowly come back into this space. Continue to breathe deeply. Gradually come back and when you open your eyes, you will feel at peace, serene, relaxed and harmonious. The water has cleared, refreshed and energized you.

CHAPTER 6

CONQUERING CHAOS

The Angels of Transparency remind me now of the state in which we exist; the world we have manifested and in which we now struggle to live. It is a chaotic world. There are wars everywhere. Mother Earth is fighting desperately, having to exert great force to overcome this chaos, to survive and to restore the natural balances. At this time, however, it is extremely difficult because mankind appears to actually want all this chaos.

The Angels tell me that now we are paying the price, affecting all aspects of our existence and our being. This chaos now manifests itself within us on both a profound physical and deep psychological level. Being in chaos is an extremely unhealthy way to live. Chaos causes people to become sick. New and old diseases are coming to life and reappearing, diseases that, even fifty years ago, where unheard of. This happened because we were busy looking at the world through different eyes. And now, because we have and want everything, chaos reigns inside us and all around us. Chaos is the cause of depression, chaos is the cause of anxiety, insomnia, chaos is also the cause of many forms of cancer; we keep getting sick because we are unfamiliar with the linearity and fluidity of the soul.

The presence of the Archangels Metatron and Michael is very strong now. Metatron appears to me as a reddish/purple light and Michael appears as a blue light. One is on my right, the other on my left. I am being shown a vision of the world split in two. One half of the world there are those people who are already 'living in the light' and on the other half there are those still living in utter darkness. The Angels of Transparency are showing me that we will be able to find inner peace by returning to the natural elements of the Earth that work to keep the energies, the life force, in harmony; the elements of fire, air, wind, and water.

The Angels now speak to me of the task of humanity on this Earth to transform the 'dark side' into a place of enlightenment. Men, whose hearts are closed, need to regenerate themselves. They are frightened children. They are just like very frightened children who experienced problems during childhood, whilst growing up, who had very strict parents, very stern parents; their fathers in particular. Therefore, by projecting 'motherly love', by giving it to everyone, these men will be able to forgive, to let go, to give love back to themselves and to others, so that this world can become a world of harmony, full of peace, light, and love.

Because this chaos is caused by human discontent, having reached a point from which no path forward can be seen; only one force can take its place - love. The keyword is 'love'. Love is unconditional, it is brotherly love and it is the love that the Light-workers will need to 'aim' at the centre of the Earth so that all people, all mankind can rise from the chaos.

The Angels of Transparency tell me we must send this love exactly to the centre of the Earth, at its fulcrum. Let us visualize a transparent Earth in front of us, with rivers, lakes, mountains, with a lot of animals and human beings. We need to return to the natural state, to our roots, to earth. We need to return to the natural elements. I see a green lawn, the people of the world living in happiness. I see waterfalls where the men of the world bathe, rivers and lakes where they drink, I see the mountains where they go to drink air, the fresh mountain air. I see the many fires where they warm up, a grand communion and brotherhood among peoples.

Archangel Metatron is guiding us in the search for this New Earth. He is astride a large golden wagon, all dressed in red, leading us across the Earth, scaling mountains and swimming freely in the oceans. We feel as though our bodies are filling with liquid energy. We journey into the Earth to reach the centre where we light a small flame of Universal Energy. A small flame of healing energy that, metaphorically speaking, is inside our own bodies; as it gradually develops and grows ever larger inside our body it becomes a fire capable of healing the world, a fire that does not burn, a fire of energy that heals all the peoples of Earth as it expands.

Expanding in this way, it gradually heals all peoples, all men and women present on Earth today, by eliminating all those elements of destruction, those problems that sicken us and Earth, like the destruction of forests. Every tree that falls is like a strong blow to our heart. The Angles of Transparency suggest we transform the falling of the tree into another action, instead of falling, we visualize the tree to swinging in the wind, and then standing up again, strong and straight. It represents our resilience to be able to stand up strong again after being, beaten down by either disease, a heavy psychological burden or at the hands of another. We rise again and continue on our journey.

Now Archangel Metatron asks us to consider the killing of animals, for their pelts, or their organs. Let us send the energy of healing to those who kill these animals, as in the case of seals those small innocent white seals. It is a crime similar to Herod's when he murdered the first born male children. It is like destroying innocence itself, the innocence inside each one of us. Instead, this innocence must always remain inside each of us, even in a mature person, in an old man or woman and in people who are continuously evolving.

And we continue to see the lights that are getting brighter by the minute, from the dark side of the orange, there are more and more lights turning on, there are more and more lights surrounding us, there are more and more lights being restored day after day. These lights have been turning on for the past twenty years.

People living in darkness are learning how to turn on their

small inner lights, those small flames that will make it possible for you to move spiritually and naturally. People will recognize each other, as today I am able to recognize people who are somewhat spiritually evolved. This evolution will lead us to loving each other with unconditional love. Not a sexual love, not a love that comes from need, but a strong, unconditional, communal love. Those who will live in this dimension will be misunderstood, but unconditional love will rule in the end.

Love and forgiveness, forgiveness and love, these are the words to remember, love and forgiveness are the cornerstones of life. Love and forgiveness, forgiveness and love. What follows is a most beautiful and powerful meditation which comes from The Angels of Transparency and is available to reignite the flame of love inside you, or to give strength to your flame when you need it. Accept this gift of love, accept yourself and others.

The Flame Of Love Meditation

Sit or lay down comfortably. Close your eyes and pay attention to your senses. Breathe deeply. Consciously inhale and exhale. Fill your lungs completely with air; feel the air go into your lungs and come out through your mouth and nose.

Each time you breathe, feel yourself become more relaxed. Inhale, pulling in to your breath, your inner energies, experience their colours and feel their warmth. Hold your breath for a few seconds, and as you exhale feel all the unwanted energy and any blockages leave your body. Keep breathing deeply.

Listen to your breath. Using your 'inner' vision see your tummy rise and fall and scan every part of your body; seeing each organ, muscle, nerve, every fibre of your physical being become relaxed. Keep breathing deeply and relax further.

Imagine your body surrounded by rings of coloured, warm light. Pay attention to your eyelids, the little muscles around your eyes and let them go. Relax your forehead and cheeks. Keep breathing deeply and steadily. Relax your lips, leave your mouth ajar. Relax your neck and shoulders by massaging them with your imagination. Caress your neck and gently flex it, allowing the shoulders to drop and relax. Your neck and shoulders are given respite from supporting the head, letting go of all tension. Continue to relax every part of your body. Keep breathing deeply, remaining mindful of your breathing and keeping your eyes closed.

Now imagine Archangel Raphael. You can see his emerald green healing ray enter your crown chakra with gentle blow. Breathe slowly and steadily as you feel his green energy pervading your body and your organs, purifying and cleansing all unwanted thoughts.

Keep breathing deeply and steadily. Now visualize a little flame inside your heart. Notice this small flame slowly and steadily grow; its light and its warmth, coming from your heart, expanding and radiating outwards to touch all your organs. Feel it touching your lungs and torso. Feel it bring light and awareness to your whole being.

Next feel the flame touching your shoulders, your hips and your upper and lower back. Now it is warming your neck, your head, your arms, your hands; to the lips of your fingers. Feel the flame touching your legs and feet, to the tips of your toes.

Feel the flame expanding outwards to illuminate your aura and at the same time witness your chakras opening to the light like beautiful, vibrant flowers. The whole of your aura is now illuminated and pulsing with the gentle healing from the flame of love. Feel this wonderful love that expands like a warm tidal wave of unconditional acceptance, touching the hearts of many, until everything it touches becomes one big heart of love.

Imagine this energetic field is completely restoring your own inner balance and sense of harmony. Now imagine this flame is all over you, around your heart, your body and your entire being. Open your arms to receive this gift of love as a present to you to share with all others. This is the real sense of living 'naturally' as was intended for us and now you feel you can experience life with greater serenity, fulfilment and with love.

Stay there for a few more minutes, enjoying the gifts of love then slowly come back into the room in this space. Keep breathing deeply. Soon, when you are told to open your eyes, you will feel a sense of peace and serenity and harmony all around you. Breathe slowly.

Visualize yourself now having been recharged, purified and cleansed by the love flame and be ready to more freely accept yourself, others and life itself. Now you can open your eyes. Gently stretch to end the meditation.

CHAPTER 7

XANTIA

The Angels say it is important for our DNA to activate fully, not just with two spirals, but with all 12 spirals. The twelve DNA spirals are those we had in the beginning, many years ago, and that lead us to a more natural way of life. Though it will be a simpler life it will be highly evolved, telepathic, an open, transparent life. It will be like widening the receiving band of a radio to tune in more channels. Soon the DNA strings will multiply; they will become four, eight, and then twelve. Many people are already receiving these messages. It is like getting to see beyond the light spectrum that we can normally see, to see in ultraviolet and infrared. There are these higher frequencies, but until now we could not perceive them. The further people evolve spiritually this change will take place.

There are 144,000 symbols hidden in our DNA, in the 12 strings of our DNA. When we are born, only one of these symbols comes to light. Metatron, who is also the Lord of the Symbols, has informed me that he has unlocked several symbols in me in order for me to gift them to humanity. The main symbol is Xantia (expressed as a cross on the heart, a commitment of love) and there will be others. The number 144 is a very spiritual number, in Biblical numerology it is the number that depicts direct spiritual guidance, and considering the word 'angel' means 'messenger' it has also been seen as the number that relates to the 'main messengers' or Archangels. It is important for people to gain a good understanding of the existence of Angels and Archangels in this world; and it is also important for Christians to learn to see Angels not only as religious figures but as guiding spirits too. This symbol is a way to unite with the Spirit.

Xantia is a very strong symbol of healing. It heals the inner-self because it is an initiation for the 'opening of the heart'. It opens the angelic chakra and balances the heart chakra. There is the number five: self, body, mind, soul, spirit. Self (centre of the universe) healed in body, mind, soul, and spirit. Things will improve once people have addressed these four elements. It is important for this to happen because Earth today is still changing, it is transforming and there is another Earth that awaits us; a land of peace, love, harmony, and brotherhood.

In conjunction with the importance of symbols, the Angels have also spoken about music. It immediately opens us up to meditation. But it needs to be a special music, both spontaneous and natural. Each symbol must have a corresponding musical chord, as does each chakra and each string of the DNA. I am currently working with the sound of whales, and dolphins to open the third eye and the chakra of the heart at the same time. This is elevated music, at the same frequency of the heart chakra; for example, music made by violins and flutes. It is important to open the chakra of the heart in order to live a simpler life.

It is vital for men to do it, in particular, because women are gentler and their heart chakras are more open. It is important for men to come into contact with certain energies, to open up to the Universal Energy, to love. Men, by their very nature, are cruder, physically stronger, and much more self-centred. The Angels of Transparency are here with me now, to open the hearts of men, of many men, in order to make contact with their souls, with their Self, so a great flow of spirituality may take place in this world. May these men feel free of social and family patterns and problems related to sexuality.

To demonstrate the impact of this symbol I will share Rose's story with you. Rose is in a circle with eight other

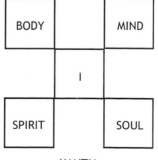

people and she is feeling a lot of different energies, but a lot of discord as well; she is torn between leaving and staying. But she decides against 'running away' feeling it would betray those who have gifted her so many opportunities in the past and have loved her unconditionally. She relaxes her mind and finds her thoughts drifting, and her journey begins.

She is inside a gothic cathedral, dancing, surrounded by beautiful stained-glass windows. While dancing, she throws herself against one of these windows and finds herself in yet another dimension, where everything has a golden light. She breathes its fresh and pure air because it makes her feel good, and her thoughts wander upwards, towards the sky. 'I know this place!' she exclaims. It is a distant time, a time that is no longer hers. Rose is filled with contradictory emotions; peaceful - restless, safe - insecure, happy - sad. She senses a desire for something new, but she doesn't know where to start!

Behold, three Angels appear majestically before Rose, telling her that they are here for everyone. They invite all humanity to board the 'train of happiness', to experience these beautiful trains that carry thousands of people around, allowing their lives to cross, embrace, and mingle. Everyone is carrying pieces of baggage that consist of feelings, wants, and hopes. Everyone is on the move! The people not on the train are running, misguidedly chasing their time as they allow the frantic pace of life to make everything look 'normal'. But if we stop and think, we realize that it is not at all like this! Normality is for those who refuse to see, who are afraid of exposing themselves and taking chances.

The Angels encourage Rose to listen or to say a few reassuring words to comfort those whom she meets on the train; it doesn't cost her a thing and helps those who receive as well as those who give. Then, at the end of the day, the train will not have travelled in vain but be full of love and it will pass through everyone's heart. Then the Angels turn to Rose, and each of them hand her a golden sword. They tell her to fight until truth triumphs. She looks at them, bewildered, is this a case of mistaken identity, why her among so many? They really are speaking to her.

Archangel Uriel takes Rose back to the time of her birth, he breathes on the little feet of that child who was born in the breech position, so that her steps may be lighter. He cuddles a little creature that would like to return to the source rather than continue to crystallize.

Rose is shown a river, having reached full capacity, it pours down as a waterfall and floods everything in its path, at times clearing the earth and at others gently meandering through the Earth it loves so much. Rose is awash with energy, she manages to relax, and listen to her heart knowing she will be free only at the end of this journey, when tears will become drops of dew and wings will replace the arms that now embrace her.

This same energy gives strength to all her senses: it improves her sight, now she can make out the images that will keep her company during moments of solitude. It strengthens her hearing that records the sounds she will hear when far from home. It enriches her sense of smell to capture the fragrances that bring back memories and it refines her sense of touch that wants to stroke everything, so as not to forget.

And then Rose is given 'Xantia', a cross on the heart, a commitment of love, a symbol branded with fire, a fire that burns from within. She would like to rejoice; instead she feels that this will be another difficult test to overcome. A voice tells her to let go of her anger, it is blinding. She must replace her desire to reason with heartfelt love. The Angels call her, the star, and the light, the rock, carried by a beam of light. A light that everyone will want to see, it will shine upon the Earth to create a trail to walk on, leaving children to play while men and women will only be capable of love. Rose says a prayer, a simple prayer that comes from the heart, 'I hope that He is listening to me. The Angels pick my words as flowers in a field and whisper to me that faith always pays. There is no power greater than prayer.'

She feels bad for having hesitated, she would like to know more and becomes totally immersed in what is passing before her and exclaims, 'I recognize this! It is the story of my life.' Profound, in places it is hard to take in. She follows a trail along a road that crosses green pastures, sunflowers and fields of wheat. She sees a cottage in the distance, her father is there telling her to join him. She doesn't listen and keeps on walking. She reaches a hill and finds herself finally walking between two low walls, where people that are dear to her sit, all of them extend their arms, but she doesn't stop and keeps on walking. She reaches a desert and crosses it. In the end she reaches the sea. The waves aren't coming ashore, but are moving in the opposite direction. She walks in, allowing the vastness of the sea to embrace her.

Now, though Rose says she still feels pleasantly uneasy with Xantia, she does believe that she is a messenger of light and together with the Angels she can change her daily routine and once again discover a surprising tranquility.

The Hologram Meditation

I want to terminate, remove and delete all the images that have been projected on to me by other people in every time, place or dimension

I want to terminate, remove and delete all the images that I have projected on to myself in every time, place or dimension.

Part Two

Universal Energy

CHAPTER 8

VOYAGES

Millions of spiritual creatures walk the earth unseen, both when we wake and when we sleep.

JOHN MILTON

There are great spiritual entities at work for us; transforming this Earth in order to heal it, to save all life on it. We should listen to their voices and teachings without fear and rather with trust. We should heed and embrace their voices and teachings with joy and determination, letting go of any doubts and uncertainties. That is what meditation is, for me.

Thanks to Reiki, I was able to open up to these forces and I am able to and want to share these wonderful experiences with you. I feel that when people will be ready to open their hearts, when they will be capable of understanding the evolution of their internal nature, then it will be easier to contemplate nature, as nature is the foundation of our lives. Nature is where we all live and share our existences; it is the place where we carry out our activities and where our destinies unfold. There will come a day when all on Earth will be able to contemplate silence, to contemplate love and to love unconditionally.

To prepare for this we need to dive into the world, to travel. Travelling is also an inner journey: In some places, it is possible to make contact with the energy of Mother Earth and Father Heaven and receive their gifts of healing. Even though we are spiritual beings, eternal souls crossing worlds and universes - beyond the boundaries that we are able to perceive in our ordinary lives, in this life, we humans must nevertheless live and experience the universal energy within a physical body on Earth.

Our task is to return to the universal unity by restoring our consciousness to its original state. The spirit takes shape in matter, and here our nature of human beings can reach illumination and happiness. We need to get to know our body well, experiment with the potential of our mind and rebalance our energy to gain health. Chakras are the connection points between spirit, soul, mind, and body so by rebalancing and healing them we can once again find our psychophysical balance.

Even Earth, formed by the meeting of Spirit and Matter, is a living being, it has a soul and a body, a mind and thought, bones and blood, a conscience and sensitivity. And it has its own chakras as well. Given the law of analogy between the micro- and macrocosm, on Earth there are special energy points as in the human body, here one can find vortexes and passages that push the energy flows upwards and downwards, inside and outwards. These are the intersection points of cosmic energy and the energy that takes shape in Earth and in matter.

These are passage and transformation points that take on the shape of special places loaded with energy: waterfalls, mountains, rocks, forests. These chakras of the Earth can rebalance our own chakras, like the heart chakra being one of the most important because it is our emotional home. In my research I discovered that the renowned town of Sedona, at the centre of the Rocky Mountains of Arizona, is the home of the heart chakra on Earth. It was no coincidence that I became a Reiki master precisely in that town; it is a point that energizes our being, even when simply meditating on the rocks for a few moments, it is where the vibrations of the chakra of the heart can be felt in all their power.

In Earth's chakras it is possible to feel the flow of universal energy and to resonate with it. Sanctuaries, where sacred ceremonies were once celebrated, were built in these ancient places: from the Eleusinian Mysteries of ancient Greece to the Druidic rituals at Stonehenge and Glastonbury in England, to the dances of the Native Americans, to the ceremonies that took place at places of apparitions in Italy, from Varanasi in India to the Holy Land, the sacredness of creation has always been celebrated.

Italy, my homeland, has many special places as well where it is possible to directly receive the help of cosmic energy and discover our connection with the All; examples of which are the places consecrated to Saint Michael the Archangel, the Spiritual Being that is guiding this era of transformation and struggle to come out of the darkness, as well as Assisi, where peace and serenity reign, as characterized by the philosophy of Saint Francis.

There are many other places like these everywhere. Little by little we should be able to discover and nourish our connection to the energies that reveal themselves. It is our nature as humans that requires it. To evolve spiritually we need to connect to these energies that can heal us and lead us to a higher plane of consciousness. It is also how we can cooperate to keep the planet in balance, just as the most spiritually evolved animals do; in the ocean there are whales, on dry land there are elephants; with the energy created by their ritual 'dances', these animals make it possible for all the chakras of the Earth to become perfectly balanced for all of us. Even we, in these sacred places, can celebrate the universal energy and receive the gifts and assistance of nature for our health. We can feel as one with Earth, with the animals, and with the plants from which we obtain the vital sap that nourishes Earth and us all. These places are where I take people to meet and celebrate the divinity of nature. These are spiritual journeys that complete my teaching, to open up even more to the flow and blessings of Universal Energy.

Because the world in which we live is currently saturated with hostility and lacks compassion it has become a breeding ground for envy and jealousy. How can we transform this heavy and negative energy into a beautiful energy of peace and tranquility?

How can we help each other live more serene, happier lives? First of all, it is very important to find our inner peace. When we are at peace with ourselves we are at peace with the world that surrounds us. It often happens that someone approaches you to project all their problems on to you. Or they pay you a compliment that is not really sincere, about the way you are dressed or how delighted they are that you had a great holiday. Then at the end of the encounter, when you bid farewell, you feel tired and drained, whereas the other person trots away happy and content that they were able to talk to you. These people are the so-called 'energy vampires', those who suck all the energy while they talk to you; you are not prepared to receive their comments and their words and, caught by surprise, you don't know what to do.

Here is what happens. These thoughts simply penetrate your aura and then your person. Besides being an electromagnetic field, the aura is like spongy matter in which all thoughts can become trapped. Over time, these negative thoughts also invade the body and become one of the negative energy clusters that little by little lead us to become that individual that other people want us to be. Let me explain: if a person meets you and pays you a compliment that is insincere, then you can become the exact image that the other person wants you to become.

Every thought is energy and every type of energy influences your aura and your thoughts. Many of those involved in energy treatments realize that if the mind sends disharmonious messages, of acrimony and hate, we become exactly what those messages told us to be: the energy clusters form in the aura at first, then in the body, and can become actual spots on your body. The energy first embeds itself in the aura, then transfers to the body and affects the physical cells to become a disease.

This is why meditation is important. This is why prayer is important. It is essential to clean one's aura every day to protect against 'energetic' attacks by means of purification. It is important to make daily contact with one's inner self and with our super-consciousness, to entertain an open dialogue with ourselves, to clean out the aura and organs and give them love and peace. There are a few simple exercises that we can do before leaving our homes. One is to visualize ourselves in a mirror, so that everything other people will tell us will reflect outwards and not affect us at all. Or, for those with the second level of Reiki, you can visualize the purification symbol all around yourself. The following meditation takes the simple form of two affirmations that are to be repeated as often as you feel comfortable and are designed to help erase these negative thoughts from your aura.

CHAPTER 9

AURAS & CHAKRAS

Our physical body: the medium, through which our consciousness is expressed, represents the lowest level of energy vibration. Our emotional, mental and spiritual elements, of which we may not be aware, vibrate at higher frequencies than the physical body. Through our physical bodies we experienced physical movement, awareness of body parts and functions, touch, taste, smell, sight, hearing and interaction with nature including earth and water elements.

Through our emotions we experience compassion, love, fear, doubt, the need for self-expression; opening ourselves up to joy and happiness. On the mental level, we use our conscious minds to think, plan, evaluate, and express ideas and articulate desires such as the desire for inner peace. The spiritual element focuses on the evolution of the soul.

Energy centres called Chakras (which means 'wheel' in Sanskrit), are located in the body, and link these four different levels together. The Chakras link an organ, group of organs or a physical part of the body to higher levels of being. The flow of energy is adapted from pure spirit to physical manifestation. When the Chakras become unbalanced or blocked, various conditions can result ranging from phobias, fears and mental ailments right through to physical pain and suffering.

The etheric body functions with the help of seven major energy gateways called chakras (there is now a belief there may be up to 13 chakras in all, but we will concentrate on the work of the most commonly known ones). Each chakra has a different colours and spinning directions, according to my studies and research. The chakras link an organ, or group of organs or a physical part of the body to higher levels of being. The flow of energy is adapted from pure spirit to physical manifestation. When the chakras become unbalanced or blocked, various conditions can result ranging from phobias, fears, and mental ailments right through to physical pain and suffering.

We will concentrate on the major seven chakras; Root, Sacral, Solar Plexus, Heart, Throat, Third Eye and Crown. They start from the bottom of the person all the way up to the head. Each chakra is like seven different beautiful coloured flowers. They need to be closed all the time. When we do any kind of energy work the chakras open like a flower blossom. In the middle of the chakra there is a wheel that rotates clockwise or anticlockwise according to the position of where they are and whether we are male or female.

If the wheel does not rotate for a while or it stops altogether and we do not do any energy work to let it turn again we experience, tiredness and fatigue up to the point when we fall ill. It looks like our flower petals get burnt out I see them slowly dying or losing their strength, that is why we need to keep up the good work in energy work and daily meditation. To get the wheel to rotate daily and not to get those flowers petals stained by stuck energy. Energy that does not flow becomes stagnant energy, stuck energy on the chakras that expanding from the outside infects the colours of the aura, that is why sometime we are missing of some colours in the energy field, because the chakras are getting tired and stop working.

Each living thing has an electro magnetic field around it. In my Reiki teachings for instance one of the first things I say when speaking of the aura is to observe the aura of the leaves on the trees. That is the first aura that you might see. Loosening the focus of your eyes, you might see a white layer of energy around leaves, tree branches and every living thing. There is energy around inanimate objects as well. When we are in a room we try to organize it so that we feel how the energy flows in a good way.

Especially if we need to do some kind of energy work in that room, like teaching a Reiki class for instance.

The aura and the chakras are working together to create the perfect harmony for the body. While observing people's auras, it is obvious if colours are missing. If there is one missing, orange for instance, what does that mean? First of all, I am aware of that colour missing, from the spectrum of the seven colours of the aura, then I realize that there is either a pale orange colour or that colour I cannot see at all. It means that the chakra has stopped spinning and while stopping has drained all the energy of the Second chakra with it so that there is no more power in that area no energy force, nothing that helps that area to come to life. Only with a Healing session we can balance that energy and make sure that the Chakra starts spinning again to re-establish a certain strong orange colour of the aura itself.

When the body has an imbalance it means that the person is becoming ill. Healers believe that when the mind starts receiving messages of frustration, depression and desperation through the aura and slowing down of the chakras then the body starts feeling it, becoming tired and letting the immune system get weak and vulnerable. That is why chakras and aura is all 'one' energy that talk to one another allowing the body to heal itself when the energy is flowing properly and there are no impediments stopping that powerful breeze.

CHAPTER 10

ARCHANGELS & THE CHAKRAS

A soul is never without the escort of angels, these illuminated beings know very well that our soul has more value than the whole world.
BERNARDO DI CHIARAVALLE

Before I explain the relationship between the Archangels and the chakras I would like to take this opportunity to share with you Sophia's story. It makes a good introduction to the importance and impact of connecting with our internal power sources. What follows is her personal account of such an experience.

"My name is Sophia. When I met Mr Vivo for the first time, my initial impression was like meeting an old soul - an angelic being. When I shook his hand I felt a strong energy flow through me. I felt at peace, in harmony, and a sense of unconditional love; all things that I had never experienced before in another human being. For me it felt like 'pure love'.

Mr Vivo came to the centre, where I was working, to talk about the work that he was about to undertake for the next four weeks - The Archangelic Meditations. With great enthusiasm I enrolled. I had been very attracted to the Angels since I was a little child and I had found now someone that did not think I was out of my mind, but that could help me to speak and connect with my Guardian Angels.

The day came. The room was prepared with soothing music and incense. Mr Vivo told us to start breathing to get the energy moving. All of a sudden I was gone. I could not hear his voice anymore, I felt pampered and cradled – like I was being carried on the wings of an angel. I had completely lost touch with my

70

body and I could see myself coming out of my body and hovering above it. I then felt the presence of two immense wings next to me. It was one of the Archangels and I felt imbued by a great love.

I could now hear Mr Vivo's voice who was guiding us through a meditation. I saw many little lights that formed an entire body just before me. It was a beautiful angel, just standing there before me, smiling at me and sending great sensations of love to my heart. It was a great emotion and a unique experience that I will cherish for the rest of my life.

Mr Vivo then took us into the second part of the meditation the one where we need to clear the chakras in order to get the Archangelic beings inside us to heal ourselves. As we were working to get the throat chakra cleared for instance, I heard a sword trespassing my throat, like I had had something stuck in there for eons and that now was ready to come out and me feeling finally free. I woke slowly from this beautiful journey, and the first person I met when I woke up was Gaetano.

I have a very strong feeling that he has come on the planet to spread his knowledge and his pure unconditional love to all the people who feel drawn to him. That same night at home, once my chakras had been completely cleared, I woke up all of a sudden, and I saw hundreds of little lights there with me. It was a magnificent show and I looked at them just like looking at a sky filled with the most luminous stars."

Now I would like to explain the role of the chakras and the Archangels who have been charged to help us to work with them at this time. The first chakra is known as the 'Root Chakra'. It is represented by the colour 'red' and relates to the first working day of the week – Monday. It is linked to Archangel Gabriel (the only 'female' among the main Archangels) and delivers the virtues of 'purity' and 'harmony'. Archangel Gabriel carries light to the Root Chakra with purity, order, hope, joy and discipline. When we feel the need to join the divine conscience through the purity of the body, mind and spirit Archangel Gabriel helps us to reawaken Kundalini in order to achieve it.

Gabriel is the Archangel of the 'Annunciation' - the messenger and can be recognized by the trumpet she carries. The feeling is one of being called to the House of the Father, and the need to balance the Karma to arrive illuminated at the House. Gabriel suggests to the spiritual pupils the importance of the acquaintance. She, moreover, remembers to maintain the Light and being servant of the Light while one becomes themselves master of the Light.

The second chakra is known as the 'Sacral Chakra'; it is represented by the colour 'orange' and relates to the second working day - Tuesday. It is linked to Archangel Zadkiel and assists with exploring 'freedom', 'transformation' and 'transmutation'. He works entirely for freedom, joy, forgiveness, alchemy, justice, transformation and liberation of the spirit. Zadkiel brings changes between us and Gaia, Mother Earth, through conscience that will help us for the next events of the renewal of the planet. Using the violet flame of the Archangels, we can ask to delete old memories, to forgive and live in the spirit of joy. Zadkiel helps us to purify our karma and to carry new vitality to our life.

The third chakra is the 'Solar Plexus Chakra', it is represented by the colour 'yellow' and relates to the middle of the working week – Wednesday. It is linked to Archangel Uriel and relates to being at 'peace' and being in 'service'. Uriel works to carry vibrations of peace and brotherhood. He helps us to bring to terms situations in our life. Uriel the Archangel tells us to assert that God is within our truth.

The 'Heart Chakra' is the fourth chakra and it is represented by the colour green and relates to Thursday. It is linked to Archangel Chamuel and carries the virtues of 'love', 'adoration' and 'gratitude'. Archangel Chamuel works to re-unite the spirits to develop the heart chakra and to send love to any relative issue of the heart: compassion, better communication, love balanced in the same comparisons of us and the others, the creation of beauty towards the limbs. The healing for the loss of beloveds and friends can carry joy in our hearts with the help of the Angels.

The fifth chakra is known as the 'Throat Chakra', it is represented by the colour 'blue' and relates to the last week day – Friday. It is linked to Archangel Michael. It governs areas related to 'protection', 'communication', 'creativity' and 'sexuality'. The name of the Archangel Michael means 'He who is like God'. He is considered the Angel that removes evil from Earth. Michael assists the purification and strengthens the chakra of the throat. The blue beam assists us in the physical and spiritual protection, when there is a need to focus the own attention on a particular plan or the own mission on the Earth. They can be invoked in order to recover the own spirit from present difficulties and traumas of the past. Michael can be called upon for protection. At night before going to sleep, after having recited the words of the hologram meditation to clear your aura, you can ask Archangel Michael to protect you during your sleep, to stay with you all night long so that your sleep will be serene and tranquil.

One of the most important things you can do is to ask Archangel Michael to cut the energetic cords with the people you have interacted with during the day, so that your energy stays pure and intact without having any debris, or energetic thoughts coming from any of the persons you have met during the day. Ask Archangel Michael to cut using his sword all the cords from people, and go to sleep safely and full of love energy.

The sixth chakra is known as the 'Third Eye Chakra', it is represented by the colour 'purple' and relates to the last working day – Saturday. Its divine link is to the Archangel Raphael and The Virgin Mary. These two powerful entities work with the students in order to open their third eye. This chakra works with the grand vision, the truth, religion and science, maintaining in itself the concept of 'immaculate conception' and desire to manifest abundance on the Earth.

The seventh chakra is known as the 'Crown Chakra'; it is represented by the colour 'white' and relates to the last day of the week, the day of rest – Sunday. Archangel Metatron, known also as 'the voice of God', governs this chakra. He carries aid with wisdom, acquaintance, inspiration, discernment and discrimination to the person. We can ask help from him to have greater brightness in the own mind for the realization of plans or knowledge like resolving a conflict. Metatron helps the persons who live in the ignorance and that are starting the journey of opening through spirituality.

In order for us to clear and keep the chakras balanced daily a simple Chakra meditation is needed. Daily, starting on the Monday and focusing the attention on the Monday chakra breathing in and out re-energize and balance that chakra resting your hands on it and sending to the chakra universal loving and calming energy. This is a good way to start the week.

The Archangels' Meditation

Relax completely, lay down on the floor and start breathing deeply and regularly. Forget your daily problems for a few minutes and dedicate this time only to yourself. Inhale through your nose and exhale out of your mouth.

Now call upon the presence of the five Archangels; Archangel Michael, who is going to be on your right, Archangel Raphael, who is going to be on your left, Archangel Uriel who is going to be above you, Archangel Metatron is going to be behind you and Archangel Gabriel who will stand before you.

As the Archangels are positioning themselves around you, you will now also call upon the Angels to protect you and guide you during the meditation. Feel the Angels coming down from the sky, sent by God for us now. They are here to help us during this process and are protecting us and our space.

Focus your attention on Archangel Michael, to your right. Archangel Michael has about him a striking blue energy and he holds a sword in his hands. Ask Archangel Michael to cut the energetic cords that are attached to your body. All the energetic cords to do with your past, with people that you have met, with people with whom you have had relationships, with situations that you want to eradicate from your mind.

Get the Archangel to cut all these old memories from our subconscious mind, cutting cords from the head, around the neck, on the torso, around the arms and the hands, down the hips and down the legs, all the way down to the feet, going through chins and calves. Up and down, front and back. Allow the blue ray of Archangel Michael to clear and cleanse your energy inside and out. Feel it following through you now, sweeping through you, breaking and sweeping away all unwanted connections.

Next be aware of Archangel Uriel. His beautiful yellow energy opens the crown chakra and blows healing into it. This yellow energy is warm like a ray of sunlight that pervades your body. It frees your body of the dust that the cords have left. Michael eradicated the energetic cords, leaving dust particles in the organs and so Uriel can now blow them away.

Your body transforms from opaque to being completely transparent, like glass, and you are healing. While Michael and Uriel are working together to clear and cleanse your aura and your body so that it becomes lighter and brighter, turn your attention to Raphael, the healing Archangel.

Raphael is bathed in green light and you now visualize this Archangel entering your body from behind, unzipping you and climbing inside to restore you and ensure that your heart is completely healed. Your heart now becomes Raphael's heart and his task is to heal it, first and foremost.

In your heart resides your inner child. It is your child that you now must get in touch with. With the help of Raphael you will try to heal the inner child. First acknowledge your inner child. Smile and him/her, to let this child know that you are here and that you have not forgotten about it. Your inner child may feel abandoned, lonely and cold. You have returned to be with him/her, to embrace this child and to ask for his/her forgiveness. Envelope the child in warm light.

Do this now by extending your hand to the child, ensuring that it remains with you, acknowledging you, hugging you in an eternal loving embrace. Asking for forgiveness, you and the child cry together, ensuring that from now on you will be as one – to grow up together and to speak to one another on a daily basis. You will feed the child with words of joy, harmony and love forever.

To be truly transparent we need to forgive and be forgiven. Raphael, who is in our heart, helps the inner child to heal. Archangel Raphael is in your heart with his emerald green ray and gives you warm, harmony, brotherhood and a great inner self-love.

Call upon Archangel Metatron now – guardian of our third

eye. He comes down with a strong purple light. He is behind us and slowly from behind he plants a little seed in our third eye that, with the help of the universal energy of love, grows 'til it becomes the 'Plant of Illumination'; a beautiful opening of the invisible things. With this plant you can start seeing the elemental beings, the crystal beings, the angels and feel a great embrace of the presence of all those beings of the invisible world. It becomes stronger and the awareness plant flourishes around you. The plant that from the earth grows towards the sky and makes you feel a great sense of joy as you are able to tap into God's vibration.

Then turn your attention to Archangel Gabriel, the messenger. Gabriel, who is standing before us, with her message of love in our hearts. It is a message for you and for all of those like you that are blossoming and growing into the new Earth into the new dimension of compassion, Great Understanding and Infinite Love.

Keep breathing deeply and slowly while the five Archangels keep working for you, through you, around you. They're helping you to feel more universal energy and compassion. Keep breathing, feeling relaxed with a great inner joy. Keep feeling their energy fill you up, purify your being, cleanse every cell of your body and clean you aura and your chakras. Now thank the Archangels that have been with you, that have helping you through this journey, knowing that any time you need their presence or need to feel them, you can call upon them and they will be with you.

You can now open your eyes and sense around you great joy and peace that permeates your entire being.

CHAPTER 11

THE POWER OF LOVE

REI = The Higher Source that controls the Universe, its creation and movements. Rei is a part of everything, infinite in nature and all knowing. It acts as a source of guidance to help in times of need. Rei is also called God, or other names depending on the culture.

KI = The Energy that radiates from, and nourishes all living things. It is essentially the life force itself, which makes up the aura. We receive Ki from food, sunshine, air and sleep. It is equivalent to the 'Chi' of the Chinese, the 'Prana' of the Hindus, the Baraka of the Muslims, the 'Orenda' of the Iroquois Indians and has many other forms. The flow of Ki provides the healthy condition of the body and obstructions to this flow can lead to illness.

Reiki is about, well-being, healing and positive energy - but above all, Reiki is about 'Love'. Reiki enhances the love that springs from our hearts and exists within and around us at all times. Reiki is a heart-centred technique that can help us to be at peace with ourselves and the world around us.

We live in a world that is beset with troubles - war, terrorism, bankruptcies - all adding to the emotional and psychological stresses of our personal and professional lives, tainting the beauty of our natural heart energy. Reiki can help us to rid ourselves of unwanted energies and focus on the pure and beautiful energy of the heart. Whether we're suffering from pressures at work, heartbreak or the loss of a loved one, Reiki holds the power to transform and bring the power of love back into our lives. This lies at the heart of my work and what I am trying to achieve with Reiki.

I found Reiki at a particularly difficult time in my life. I was at a complete standstill, beset by stagnation, with no idea of where to turn. I was lost in this maelstrom when the 'hand of fate' intervened and I met with an amazing person who introduced me to the wonders of Reiki. The experience was deeply transformational and changed my life profoundly. Ever since I have sought to pass on the healing power and benefits of Reiki to the people I meet who live their lives surrounded by fear; fear of crime, fear of losing those they love, fear of death, and fear of simply existing and living in this world. And as a result, people withdraw from everything, from the world, and from themselves. To protect themselves, they insulate their feelings and their hearts. They block off their heart chakras and the beautiful healing energy that springs from the heart and from love. It is essential to have an open heart and to help as many people in the world as possible - but how can you help others if you can't help yourself?

Reiki can help us open up and clear these energy flows, freeing up the positive healing energy of our hearts and bringing love back into our lives. It helps us focus on love - the love within us, and the love that surrounds us. Once we learn to recognize the love within ourselves, we achieve an equilibrium that allows us to exist at peace with ourselves and the world around us. That in turn allows us to look beyond the self and help those around us.

Understanding Reiki as an expression of love can help us clean the clutter from our lives - clearing up our hearts and minds to do great good. It is through harnessing this healing energy that Reiki is able to ease emotional, mental and physical ailments. For example the healing power of Reiki as love can be illustrated by the manner in which Reiki is said to be able to ease the process of childbirth, bringing mother and child closer together, by sharing the beautiful energy of the heart chakra, enabling a more natural childbirth.

Reiki is a spiritual practice which harnesses healing energy to restore balance in the body, mind and spirit. By definition, Reiki means 'Universal Life Force Energy' - the 'ki' that moves through and around all living things. A Reiki Master or practitioner harnesses this energy by laying his or her hands on the body, channelling the energy to balance the chakras, restoring a sense of wellbeing. The laying of hands on the human body is not a new concept. If pain is experienced, or children injure themselves, the first thing we are inclined to do is to put our hands on the affected area, to 'make it better'. Human touch provides warmth and feelings of caring and love, and many therapies incorporate touch as part of the healing process. And this 'healing' is not just the removal of the symptoms, as is commonly thought. Healing is a complete process and fully resolves the cause of ill health. With healing you are returned to the state of alignment with your 'higher self' - your true way of being. Once the chakras are balanced, excess energy that we do not need rises to the surface, allowing the Reiki practitioner to draw it out of the body, clearing the way for new clean and pure energy to flow.

I have one regular client - a lady who comes to see me every fortnight. Her marriage recently ended and the heartbreak of the break-up was causing her much emotional and mental trauma. From the moment she enters the therapy room - a clear space with soothing music and the relaxing aromas of incense and perfumed oils - she can feel herself relaxing. As the Reiki treatment begins and I lay my hands on her, she is visibly overwhelmed, her eyes overflowing with tears. This excess energy rises to the surface and is drawn away, while her healing heart energy envelops her. From her first session, she tells me, she has already started seeing the world around her and inter-acting with her surroundings in a more positive manner. And, she says, with every visit, she learns a little more about herself and feels more well-being. She now says she understands people more and feels at peace with herself and with Nature. Fundamentally she has understood that if she is unable to love herself, she cannot love others.

I believe that Reiki is amongst the purest expressions of love. As such, I like to concentrate on the energy flowing from the heart chakra, focusing on bringing back that love, love for one's self and bringing back love for other people. This healing energy can then be used to bring emotional and mental ease or even help with physical ailments. Originally developed by Buddhist monks in Tibet, Reiki has now been adopted in the western world and is used to treat a number of different ailments, both mental and physical. Reiki is one of the greatest gifts you can receive and share with others. Reiki is universal love, compassion, harmony and balance. This leads to feelings of power and a sense of wholeness - the path to joy and happiness.

The person who is a Reiki practitioner (or healer) receives an 'attunement', which opens the energy channels of the body and clears any obstructions in the flow of Ki. The attunement also connects the practitioner to the source of the Universal Energy, for life. The connection to the source and the ability to channel the energy is further enhanced with additional attunements. To connect with the Reiki energy the receiver places the hands upon himself/ herself or on others, and the energy will flow through him/her automatically.

Since Reiki is guided by a 'Higher Intelligence', the mind and experience of the practitioner does not affect the Reiki energy. The mind of the client does not affect the healing energy, whether or not they believe in Reiki. The energy knows where to go and what to do. The person giving Reiki experiences an increase in Ki, often feels energized and can perform several healing sessions in succession. The energies of the practitioner are never depleted, as the Reiki energy is channelled. Reiki always provides healing, is always positive and, from my experience, everybody benefits from its use.

Typically, one session of Reiki lasts between 60 - 90 minutes. However, one session is rarely sufficient. Once you've received healing energy from the heart chakra, it is important to continue with regular sessions - once a week or so - to perpetuate the healing process, allowing you to truly appreciate and understand the healing energy, to come to terms with the upheavals in your life and move forward healed and whole.

A Reiki treatment involves placing the hands in a number of standard positions on the body, front and back, including the head and the feet. Some of the positions correspond to the energy centres called chakras, which regulate the healing energy to the body. Additional positions may be used for a specific condition affecting the client. Each hand position is held for approximately 3 minutes, but can be more or less depending on the needs of the particular person.

The client lies fully clothed on a treatment table, and the Reiki session may include a discussion during which the practitioner determines any special requirements for the healing. The treatment radiates a deeply relaxing and calming sensation that benefits both the client and the practitioner. The experience varies with each session and is unique to each person. People describe the Reiki energy as heat, warmth, coldness, feelings of dizziness or electricity, and some even feel nothing at all. This does not mean that they are not receiving any energy, but that they will feel the effects of Reiki at a later stage. Once attuned to the energy, you can also treat yourself, by placing your hands on your body.

Once people have experienced the beauty and power of the love and energy that flow from the heart chakra, most people want to receive more – as well as share this love with those around them. This is why many recipients of Reiki desire to learn it, so that they are able to pass on the benefits. It experiencing and understanding the power of Reiki that led me to practise Reiki. I have now been practising Reiki for over a decade and still I find

I continue to grow and learn - about myself, the universe and the healing power of Reiki and love.

Reiki will heal the cause of a problem on whatever level it may exist - mind, body or spirit, as the Ki in the body can also be affected by thoughts and feelings. Negative thoughts and feelings are the main cause of restrictions to the flow of Ki. This is supported by the fact that the mind is responsible for many illnesses in the western world. Reiki can work directly with the unconscious mind that contains these thoughts and feelings, breaking them up and washing them away. The Ki is then allowed to flow freely, balancing the function of the physical body and restoring the healthy condition.

If you think of your body as a house full of lights, the attunement process is similar to the act of turning on the electricity. The electrical switches connecting to the lights represent the chakras or energy centres in the body. The chakras link our physical bodies to our 'higher spiritual-self'. These switches require repairing and need to be tested, to ensure that there are no blockages to the flow of electricity. In the same way the chakras in our body need to be balanced for the Ki to flow correctly. Once the switches (chakras) are cleared of obstructions the electricity itself (Reiki Energy) is able to flow freely and make your house (body) light up!

After being attuned, each individual will be in contact with, and receive assistance from Reiki spirit guides. Some of these guides will remain for a long time (even for life) while others may be with you only for a short period. In a healing session, as soon as the energy begins to flow, your guides will appear, and assist if required. Reiki guides may be Saints, Ascended Masters, Angels and Archangels, friends and family, animal spirits or beings from other planets and dimensions.

As in other forms of healing, a Reiki practitioner can provide absent healing, with the use of a secret symbol, to another person in another location. The symbol, takes the energy to a higher level, such that the hands are no longer required to touch the physical body to provide healing. Reiki is both powerful and gentle. Reiki can be used as a preventative treatment as well as restoring the body to its full level of health. The healing can be applied either for physical or mental ailments. It helps boost the immune system, which aids the body in curing itself.

Reiki can reduce or eliminate physical pain and has aided healing skin problems, cuts, headaches and migraines, colds, flu and back pain. Reiki can also be used to relieve stress, insomnia, lack of self confidence, anxiety, to overcome unwanted habits and to protect from harm. Plants, animals and even machinery respond well to Reiki. Reiki flows into animals in the same way as it does in people, healing all ailments. Plants can grow stronger, and develop new buds and blossoms, and even seeds can be empowered with Reiki energy. Hands can be placed on mechanical equipment to remove faults and improve the working condition.

The ability to use Reiki is transferred to the student through attunements. The attunement is about rediscovering something that has always been a part of us, but with which we lost the ability to connect. Anyone can learn Reiki, and it is not necessary to have previous experience or ability. The attunement process opens the heart and crown chakras and provides a direct link between the student and the Universal Source of Reiki Energy. After the attunement, if the student places his or her hands on somebody else with the intention of healing, the energy will automatically flow from the student to the recipient.

The teaching of Reiki is divided into three levels: a structure that reflects the very nature of the human being (body-mind-spirit). The first level is devoted to learning ways to help the well-being on physical level. The second level is more powerful is concerned with the welfare of the mind. It enables to us to connect with our higher consciousness (the spiritual sphere), to ensure that our issues are raised and resolved, such as depression, insomnia, abuse and addiction.

At the second level Reiki we learn three sacred symbols that serve as a guide to increase the flow of energy. Drawing the symbols three times in the air beside the body of one who receives Reiki (or treatments from a distance) and repeating the mantra mentally increase considerably the power of Reiki. The energy that activates the symbols can be received only by a Reiki Master, otherwise the symbols themselves have no value. Many say that the symbols must remain secret, but I totally disagree. This could have been appropriate at the times of Mrs. Takata (though a controversial figure, she is nonetheless credited with bringing Reiki to the Western World), but not now where everything is in constant evolution, and you can see all sorts of symbols on the internet, so the best way is to know the symbols well and to learn to draw them in the right way.

It is most important that the students who approach the learning of Second Level Reiki know the symbols well rather than just trying to remember how to draw them. Reiki as we know is to give love to ourselves and to others. However, especially when we do it ourselves, it is important to establish close contact with our body. That's why during the self-treatment I always recommend my students to talk to their bodies, asking them if they are well and leave a response to flow with an open heart to accept them.

I should like to share with you what I teach at this point. You should begin by focusing your attention on the heart chakra. Put your hands on the heart chakra; first the right and the left to receive the Universal Energy within us. It's like pressing on a button so we can listen to the flow of energy from the source of life within us. Slowly and gently, moving one hand at a time, place your hands on your face, giving all the energy of the Universe into your cheeks and then your mouth allowing it to flow through your teeth and jaws. Give energy to this part of your body for at least a full minute.

Next move your hands to your eyes. Now visualize yourself from birth to the end or your days. Thank the eyes for allowing you to do so. Rest your hands on our eyes and feel the energy flow into them. Pause there for a few seconds and then slowly place your hands to our ears. Thanking the ears that allow us to hear.

Slowly place one hand on your neck and the other on the throat. Give energy to the throat chakra in front and behind, the vocal cords and thyroid. Let your other hand rest on the neck. Working on the neck work on the cerebellum, which helps with muscles and with voluntary movements, and slowly move the hand from the throat to the forehead and give energy to your brain, which is the home of our thoughts, our mind, but also to the central nervous system. It is also the home of the glands that are located in the brain, such as the pituitary. Give love to the brain and thank it for the help it gives in your life. Send loving messages to your brain, putting both hands on your head, one at a time, with gentleness and kindness to inundate the crown chakra and the whole brain of white, strong energy.

From the head, move the hands, one by one, on to the chest - the home of the heart chakra, the home of feelings. This energy that you give to your heart makes you feel good about yourself and others. Visualize an emerald green energy that pervades the entire area of the heart, the breast glands that are located in this area, such as the thyroid and the thymus. By giving love to this part of the body, we give energy even to our lungs.

Now move your hands down to the base of your rib cage - the solar plexus chakra. This is the home of emotions, negative ones such as anxiety, thoughts of hopelessness, negative thoughts, but also positive ones. The Indians call it the 'city of jewels' and the Japanese refer to it as our 'second brain'. Rest your hands on your body and feel the energy flow in our organs, such as the stomach, the liver, the pancreas, the kidneys, and all the other organs located in this area. Let you hands move around the body, front and back.

Now put your hands on the sacral chakra, a few inches below the navel. Fill the colon and the organs close to it of this magnificent orange energy, feel the smooth functioning of all organs. This chakra is the house of sexuality, communication and creativity, and has close links with the throat chakra (these two chakras are the Yin and Yang chakra). So as you give loving thoughts to the sacral chakra you also fill all of the body with a great sense of peace and relaxation.

Finally place your hands on the root chakra which is located at the base of the spine. This chakra allows us to be rooted to the Earth. We give energy to our legs, we thank them daily that they keep us walking, running, jumping, thanking them to support the full weight of our body. It helps you daily to move forward in life. After giving so much love to our body, thank it for all the things that it allows you to do and to keep sending you signals of love so that you will be living a more peaceful existence.

Nowadays, I teach classes for Reiki level 1 and 2 regularly all over the world. My Reiki level 3 course is more complex and I only teach it to people who really wish to explore Reiki at a deeper level and want to enhance their spiritual journey. My Reiki level 3 class takes a few years to complete. To give you further insight or a taste of what a class involves, a typical Reiki level 1 class, starts with registration and then 'smudging' the new students to clearing their auras. The art of smudging comes from the Native Americans. Smudge sticks are usually leaves of sage, rosemary or other healing herbs, which are put together in a bundle, burning them produces a nice smell of smoked herbs and it is very powerful to clean people's aura, to clean a room, a crystal, to actually purify everything around us and ourselves. Then we sit in circle and I start asking the students to introduce themselves and to tell us their experience with Reiki.

In my Reiki I & 2 classes there are also some of my Reiki 3 students, participating in the classes with me is part of their

Reiki Master training. They are very supportive not only of me but also of the new students that are preparing for this new experience. After introductions, I present myself. Though most students have already some knowledge of me, because they have heard my name somewhere, or they have consulted my website, I think it is important for the new students to know about me from my voice, my point of view on to things and my previous experiences with my Reiki Mission.

Then I present Reiki. I usually start by clarifying that Reiki is not a religion. It has occurred to me, especially when I teach classes in Italy, which is a country where 95% of the population is Roman Catholic, that people think that studying Reiki goes against their reliogious beliefs and credo, this is not so. Reiki is only a platonic form of love. It is love that we give to ourselves and others, nothing else. I feel that people have lost that sense of seeing Reiki as love. Neither is Reiki a 'massage'. Some people believe that they come to learn the 'Reiki Massage'. Reiki is a touch of love. It happens without any manipulation; people are fully clothed. Then we meditate and I go on to explain the role of the chakras.

We have a break and I ask the students to leave the room, as I energetically prepare the room again for the Reiki attunements, usually my Reiki 3 students help me as part of their training to clear the room from unwanted energies, using Reiki symbols and smudging sticks. I prepare the room so that when the students come in, they can all sit together with their back facing the middle of the circle of chairs.

They come in, and sit, and I change their seats sometimes, to balance the energy in the room, what I mean with this is, that for me, everything has to have a certain balance energetically in the room, and we all know that each individual has got its own energy, so I ask my students to exchange places with this or that student in order for the energy to flow perfectly in the room. I find this all the time to work for the best, as I start to initiate them into the Reiki energy. I call upon my Reiki Guides, my Guardian Angels, especially Archangel Michael and Archangel Metatron who are always with me, so that in the room there is always a sense of peace and high energy vibrations.

The attunements procedure lasts at least an hour, this is in accordance to how many students I am attuning. In a Reiki I or 2 class, there are four attunements, I usually give two attunements on a Saturday morning and two on Sunday morning. Usually a Reiki I or a Reiki 2 class lasts a weekend, about sixteen hours in total. During the attunements I play my chakra guided meditation so that the students can meditate, lose themselves into the music and clear their chakras at the same time.

It is always a very moving experience attuning new students, and it is even more moving when they come back from their journey and tell us all the beautiful places they have been, whom they have been with, and where have they gone. Sometime some people cannot talk soon after as they are too emotional, some others feel extremely happy, and others extremely sad. Above all there is a sense of rejuvenation and healing all over the room. I will always say a Reiki Master gets healed by his class.

After the initiations and even before they start talking, I ask them to follow my hands, as I am going to show them a self Reiki Treatment (the one I described to you earlier in this chapter) so they should remain in that meditative state of mind, because they are going to experience for the first time how you feel giving Reiki to yourself.

I never allow anyone to record my classes, because no two Reiki classes are the same. The different energies in the room, brought in by new students is different all the time, I say things differently according to the people who are in the class. I give my students manuals that they can take with them at the end of the seminar, and where they can take notes for everything I say, and ask me any questions or concerns that they may have.

We then meditate more and we give thanks to the guides who

have been with us in this process of transformation. People, who come to take Reiki Level 1, generally do it out of curiosity but they leave the class always mesmerized by what they have learned and how much they have changed. Don't ever be surprised when from the Monday morning after class, people around you, co-workers, colleagues, etc, they tell how much nicer you look, and the more time passes the more beautiful you become. It is a beauty that comes from inside, then eventually will show outside. You will also change for the better, and you will become a better person. Unwanted friends leave you and new friends will enter your world.

I never liked large classes. My classes have no more than 20 people. I want to get to know each student, and show them how they can open themselves to Reiki and how to use it for themselves first and then for others. After Reiki I or II workshop, our body needs to adjust to that experience, it is like a bomb of energy has gone off in our bodies, the body gets upside down and all sorts of thing can happen to our body, because it is so shaken, you might get constipation, diarrhoea, you might get flu, stomach ache, you might get nothing at all. It all depends on individuals and at what stage of their journey they are. The Reiki treatment, I teach and I have created, is very thorough and goes from the top of the head to toes and on the other side of the body.

It is important for the students to know that they are not going to heal anyone but themselves in the Reiki experience. The Reiki therapist is only a channel for the client that asks to be healed. When someone comes to you it is because at some level they have already decided that they want to heal. We have a lot of talking during the seminar. I allow my students to ask me all sorts of questions during and after the workshop. The seminar finishes with a closing meditation, and thanking the spirit guides for their healing support and love. Then we have the diploma ceremony and greetings.

Although at the end of a Reiki I class all the students are very enthusiastic about the seminar and they would sign up for a Reiki II workshop straight away, not everybody comes back for Reiki II. I would say that a 50% of them attend the next Reiki II seminar and a 20% more would come onto a another one. Usually a 30% of them decide not to continue for Reiki II. The Reiki III class, as I mentioned earlier takes the teachings much further. I do not agree to teach everybody, only those few students I chose to train as Reiki Master Teacher. I always tell them that there are many Reiki Master Teachers that can teach a Reiki III class in a weekend, but I cannot. My consciousness tells me that I am not able to do so over a weekend and that I should be very selective and particular about that. There are hundreds of so called Reiki Masters out there that do not know anything about Reiki.

Reiki can also heal animals and plants. To highlight this is the story of Manu, my golden retriever. Manu is a beautiful dog from England who still looks and acts like a puppy. I knew that there was a special bond between us the moment I went to buy her from a kennel outside London. I had made arrangements with the owner of the litter for a female, and he told me, 'Well, Mr. Vivo, I have only two females, so you had better hurry.' I did. When I arrived there were five beautiful Retrievers still being nurtured by their mother, and this odd little puppy came towards me, clumsy and very sweet. I took her.

Manu proved to be a gentle and kind soul from the beginning. She would follow me everywhere. When Manu was three years old I decided that I wanted her to have puppies. I took her to have eye and hip tests. She passed the eye test but unfortunately, she did not pass the hip test. The vet I was using at the time told me that Manu had a dysfunction in her hips and that she could not sustain a pregnancy because she would die during it. The vet also said that two of the bones in her hips were causing a middle bone to disintegrate, and that I would have to put her to sleep in a few months because she would begin limping and I would not want her to suffer.

I was distraught. I did not want to lose my adorable dog, and I certainly did not want to see her suffer. At that time, I had only completed Reiki level I, but I started giving treatments to Manu daily. She loved it - I was helping her with her suffering. She would lie down ready for me to give her Reiki. When she needed it. Therefore, I continued this for several months. Manu is now 9 years old; she has never limped and is a very happy and healthy dog. When I walk her, people ask me, 'How old is your puppy?' I tell them she is no longer a puppy and they can't believe it. Her spirit and soul have been a gift from heaven to me. She is my teacher and my closest friend. If I am upset, she is the first one who comes to take care of me. It will always be this way for us.

Finally, before I share my story with you, I would like to close this chapter by disclosing the very simple, but profound Reiki principles, which can be applied to all regardless of what you believe or practice. The Reiki principles state the following: *Just for today do not worry. Just for today do not anger. Honour your parents, teachers and elders, earn your money honestly and show gratitude to every living thing.*

CHAPTER 12

REVIVAL - MY JOURNEY

I grew up in Italy, raised as a non-practising catholic. My day-to-day life was quite ordinary. In the morning my sister and I would get ready for school where we would stay until one o'clock in the afternoon when Dad would come to pick us up and take us home. We would all have lunch that Mum would have prepared. My Mum was one of those great Italian 'mamas' and an extraordinary cook. At lunch we would talk about school and family matters. It was like a ritual. Then Dad would go to have his nap for two hours, and us kids had to be as quiet as mice. I remember a couple of times when my sister and I were too noisy and Dad would wake up and beat us with his belt. I would spend the afternoons with my mother and my sister, doing homework and watching TV.

Because I grew up in the company of my sister and my mother only, I had them as role-models (my father was rarely there). I grew up with veneration for my mother, I had developed a bond with her that still exists to this day, though she is no longer of this world. She used to protect me; she was my ally. Each time my Father's verbal and physical abuse got too much for me to bear, she would always be the peace-maker. She would support and encourage my studies, my work and my life. I miss her terribly. I miss talking to her, laughing with her, feeling her smile upon me.

Despite his temper, my father was a very respectable, self-made man. He had studied to become a pharmacist and had his own business. In Italy at the beginning of the 1960s, there were three important figures in the village: the priest, the doctor and the pharmacist. Dad was a very important person and people would go and ask him for advice. Dad wanted the best of everything for us, but it came at a price. He was a severe and very authoritarian father, concerned about what other people would think of him and his family. You can imagine how it was for him having a son who was 'different'.

I didn't spend any quality time with my Dad who was always too busy making money. He could have made time for his children at the weekend but he preferred to go hunting from dawn to mid afternoon, then he would come back home, have lunch, go to bed, wake up, watch football and never talk to us at all. Sometimes he would drag me along on his hunting trips. I hated it. I could not bear the thought of him killing so many birds. My mother would not cook the birds as she hated it too, so Dad would give them away to friends and relatives.

Occassionally he would bring home some injured ones and give them to me. Eighty percent of the time they would die from their injuries, but a few times I would heal them with care and love and then I would release them.

I have never had a good relationship with my father, he used to call me 'the iceberg', because I kept my distance from him and didn't want to hug or kiss him. That, actually, was only the result of his selfishness. I have always felt unwanted and not appreciated, and because of that I grew up distancing myself from him until I completely forgot that I had a father.

I was an extremely shy and introverted boy. I did not do well at school because I had a very traumatic time at the hands of my school teacher. In Italy the first five years of primary school are spent with the same teacher. 'Teacher Emma' was a repressed and frustrated woman who was so controlling that I was frightened of her. So you can imagine that at school I had this monster who would beat me for everything I would do or say wrong, and then at home I was even more frightened of my father who would do the same. I grew up lonely, feeling unwanted and miserable all the time. I would fear my own shadow, never had one friend and never wanted to go out, unless I was with my beloved sister. I had this big fear of being rejected by my teacher, by my father and by the other children at school.

I was different. I was bulled and rejected many times by the other kids. I was aloof and loved to be alone. I could not communicate well with the other kids. I was never invited to play with the other kids because I was the 'odd' one, especially growing up in a very well to do family and being so different. All that time alone, away from my peers, meant I grew up in a different way.

I had created a fantastical world around me, a world invisibile to others, where I could return each time I wanted to feel safe and secure. I remember, going to bed and seeing angels enter my room, pick me up and take me away. They showed me different countries and several other surreal places. They were preparing me, for my life. The Angels have been my teachers, my invisible brothers and sisters, those who have taught me everything in my life. They have taught me, to be sensible and sensitive, to be gentle and caring. Not to get angry, never to shout never to be upset of other people's behaviour and to forgive, always forgive people. They continue to advocate that life is beautiful; an evolutionary system of souls.

Then one night while I was talking to my angels, my father entered my room. He started questioning me. I would not answer him, so he started beating me, until I finally told him who I was talking to. I guess he was scared, or worried. It felt like I was being tortured at an inquisition. I was taken to psychologists and psychiatrists to see what was wrong with me. I went through all sorts of medical examinations to see if there was something wrong in my brain or in my body, had I caught something? The doctors could not find anything wrong with me at all. Needless to say, that all of my extra-sensory activities stopped completely.

Desperately looking for help, and being too young for an introspective journey, I found protection and satisfaction in food.

Once my channels, which allowed angelic beings into my space, had been shut down as a result of my father's brutal reaction, I would just eat and eat, and become fatter and fatter, so much so that at a later stage I developed diabetes. I have learned, since, that type 2 diabetes developes in people who don't have *joy de vivre* anymore, and in people who are not valued enough in life. Since my relationship with the angels had been taken away, the only thought I had growing up was to reach them in death.

My father has never told me, 'Well done' for anything. I have been waiting for that to happen all my life. I am no longer. I have realized that he will never say such a thing to me. He wanted his children to have university degrees. My sister and my younger brother did indeed become pharmacists, as my father wanted. But I am his 'first born' and I have not done anything that he expected of me. I am not a pharmacist, I am not married, I did not give him a grandchild, but then, whose's life is it, mine or his?

On the other hand, I have been always a great admirer of my grandfather on my mother's side. The family man. He was a builder; rather than building houses he used to build roads. I remember he would spend all week working outside Naples coming home at weekends only. I have been always been closer to my mother's family then my father's. Every June, when school broke up for the holidays, I would go and spend two weeks at my grandparent's house in Naples. It was a great joy for me as I could spend time with my aunties, my mother's sisters, and my beloved grandparents. We were very close and they would spoil me. It was the best time. A time for me to relax and be away from my parents and get spoiled by my grandparents.

There was a tradition in our family where every Saturday afternoon my grandmother and her three daughters would come to our house and together we would wait for my grandfather to come back from his week of work away from home. The wait, was a time of joy for all of us, we would cook and prepare dinner in an old-fashioned way, and us kids would help mother and aunties to prepare a great dinner for grandfather who would arrive later. When he arrived, he would get us all sorts of gifts and it was like Christmas every week.

My grandfather was a very tall and chubby man, who liked his food, in the family nowadays relatives say that I look like him. He was my ideal father, he was kind to me and he would listen to my needs and my problems. He would have smile on his face all the time. He was a healer in his own way. He would help poor people and help charity organizations all the time. I remember those times with great nostalgia. Now I only have my aunties, who somehow support my work and look at it in great admiration, just like when I was a little kid and they would take me away from home to let me spend time with them away from our family's daily problems and worries.

Not having my father's affection growing up, made me take different life choices. A lot was expected from me, but I failed all of my father's expectations. I therefore grew up with the fear of this very authoritarian and tough father. I grew up with fear of confrontation towards him or even talking to him made me nervous and numb. I could not express my sadness in front of him, I can still remember his words, 'Only women cry, you are a man, don't cry!' I felt I had to create a life by myself; without his help or anyone else's. Only listening and operating. That is the way I function now. Listening to angelic beings who are around me always and every time I need their help.

It has taken me half of my life to finally forgive my father and forgive myself to have been in those situations. Once you reach that point your heart opens so much wider that nothing can stop you to progress in your life, and that is the most beautiful time. Healing your inner child is an amazing experience, that only going through difficult times like those you realize how important you are in the Universe. When I was seventeen, my parents decided to send me to England on a summer vacation. This was the first time I would leave home alone on a summer experience with other boys and girls of my own age. I had always been very interested in this country. I did not know why, then. I had read many books on England, English Language, History and English Literature which was the subject I had always excelled at in school. I thought it would give me a sense of freedom, a sense of liberation, travelling meeting foreign people and start learning a new language.

The respect that the English have for animals and plants and their gardens it was just beyond my vivid imagination growing up, not to mention the respect that the English have for other people. It does not matter what country, what religion, what culture, what colour, what sexuality, in England everything is allowed and that gives me a strong feeling of freedom and opening my wings to fly.

I will always remember the first time I arrived in England, it seemed like going back home, and I felt like I was 'home'. I promised myself that I would take up English History at University and move to England forever, as soon as I finished my degree. So I did. I graduated in 1989 from the Oriental University, Naples with a doctorate in English Literature and History. I have never taught though, my biggest desire was to live in England. I graduated in March and in April of that year. I was already living in London, happier than ever and satisfied that I had accomplished my dream so far. I had no idea what was about to happen...

One day I decided to visit Hampton Court Palace, the residence that Cardinal Wolsey had built for his king, Henry VIII. When I arrived there, I had the greatest experience of my life. I knew I had been there before. I knew that palace inch by inch. I knew that I had been there in a previous life, at the time of Henry VIII. Was I the King? Was I a servant or was I a fool? My thesis at university had been about the Tudor period, and growing up I would only buy books on the Tudors, for some inexplicable reason. When I got to Hampton Court, the whole picture became so much clearer. I decided to get a job as a sales person in Westminster Abbey where I would sell gifts to tourists, but going to this beautiful church every day and being surrounded by such great history and literature, gave me a daily dose of inspiration..

As soon as I started living in England I began having all sorts of paranormal experiences. I felt like my third eye was opening again and I could really sense my guardian angels, my spirit guides, all directing me towards a new life, a new beginning. They had taken me to England once more and now they wanted for me to be here for quite sometime. Once I left the Abbey, I decided that I wanted to put my English language skills into practise. I started a career as a translator. That job was satisfying only to the point that I could interact with people from different countries and speaking several languages, but soon enough that job bored me to death. So I left.

With the money I had saved in my translation job, I bought a flat in Chiswick, West London. I was thrilled to have saved enough money to buy my little cosy apartment there, that I still own now. It is my sanctuary. Each time I return from travelling, the flat is my secure and safe space where I have created all this beautiful energy that allows people to relax and feel at home. After having bought the flat, I decided that I wanted to become self-employed, and having a shop or a centre was something that would give me joy and possibly peace of mind.

So I joined classes at *The College of Psychic Studies* in London, where great mediums and healers teach inspiring and interesting classes. I took up classes with Arthur Molinary, Robin Wimbow, Gerry March and Ivy Northage, on Developing Mediumship and Psychic Development. I studied the Tarot and all sorts of new things. I was very hungry of knowledge and spiritual development. I then decided to open a shop called *The Metaphysical Centre*.

I selected many different kinds of people to give readings at the centre. I was trying to approach the right kind of clientele for such an important venture. The shop would sell books, tarot cards, crystals and many other esoteric and 'new age' products. I had never been a business man before though. I had many people working for me, readers and staff, and most of them took me for a big ride. I would trust everyone, and without having someone with their feet planted firmly on the ground behind me; the shop soon suffered. I remember being seated behind the counter, people would come in looking at books, sit next to me, say how wonderful they felt and what great energy they could feel, then after being there for 5 or 10 minutes, put the books back on the shelf and leave. But people loved the shop. They enjoyed coming in and finding all sorts of soothing and enchanted material that would satisfy their needs. I would have foreign mediums and therapists, giving talks on different subjects and the shop was always full of nice and interesting people.

I fondly remember a particular lady who would come every other day, she would park the car just outside the shop; she had one of those disabled badges. She used to walk with a stick. She would come in, greet me with a wave and start reading all the books on the shelves, especially those ones that would talk about herbalism and well-being for women. She was a fascinating woman and we used to have the greatest conversations. After having browsed through the books, she would come and sit next to me, giving me advice and hints on how to run the shop more effectively. I remember learning a lot from her, and in exchange I would give her books that I knew she could not afford to buy. More than once she said, 'I come here to be in this beautiful energy you have created. It relaxes me and I feel so much better. You will see, one day you will be a great healer'. But at the time it was not what ai wanted to hear.

In the shop I was getting bored day by day, as my heart was not there anymore. So I was looking from answers from the Universe that would have made my life change completely. One day, a lady came into the shop asking me about Reiki. It was the first time I had heard that word. A few days later, I was visiting the Body Mind and Soul exhibition in London, looking for some new ideas for the Metaphysical Centre. There I met Stefanie. She was seated at her stand with a great smile and as I was passing by she asked me whether I wanted to experience ten minutes of Reiki. That word again... Was the universe telling me something? I decided to try. Stefanie gave me a treatment, which I loved. In 10 minutes she had put me in a state of complete relaxation and peace, despite being surrounded by hundreds of people. I signed up for a Reiki level 1 which she was teaching the following weekend and I became Reiki level 1 practitioner.

I felt like a big huge gateway had been opened before me. I was going on a different path and I felt like that was so true to my heart. There it was, the answer to my many questions. Everyone whom I would encounter would tell me what a great spiritual healer I was. I refused to understand, I did not like it at all. Reiki saved my life. Transformed it in so many ways that it is unbelievable to think that I am the same person that once I was.

My life was slowly changing, I started giving Reiki treatments to all the people who were working in the Centre, and they all loved it. My channels had been opened and I could feel a lot of beautiful energy coming through my crown chakra and through my body and finally to my hands. That year I went to Arizona on vacation with my companion, and there I met Shalinda, another Reiki Master who was offering a Reiki level 2 seminar and I decided to take it. A few months later, Shalinda initiated me with Reiki level 3 as well. After having undergone so major a cleansing and purification and been with her in Sedona for over a month, I went back to England with the idea of not wanting to be a business man anymore but only a Reiki practitioner. I was offering Reiki treatments at the Centre and I had a few regular clients too.

It occurred to me that as I was giving Reiki to clients, I was healing myself on all levels: Physical, Spiritual, and

Psychological, all my fears were dissipating and I was getting better by day. I could feel a sense of joy, peace in my life daily. I was getting to a stage where I no longer got angry or nervous. I had started to forgive people and to let them go from my past. I had finally forgiven my father with whom I have had always a very challenging relationship. I had forgiven myself to have allowed that in my life. I was teaching my clients to let go and to forgive as they were benefitting from the treatments I was giving them. My very low self esteem was growing daily. I had finally found something that filled my heart, something that would make my heart sing for joy.

I have never healed anyone but myself. You, dear reader, will never hear from me the sentence I have healed you, Never! It is not for me to say. Only God can heal and only the willingness of the patient. The Reiki therapist is only a medium, a channel, a go between that uses their body for the energy to be passed on to a living thing that needs help.

When we give Reiki to a patient, they come to us to receive help, if they ask, it means that they are already at a stage where they are willing to let go and to start the healing process. We are only here to help them. When I give a Reiki treatment, I feel like the unwanted energy the so called 'negative energy' leaves the body of the client, there is a shift of energy happening from head to toe. It is like a great mass of energy that does not need to be there anymore leaves the body from the feet, and the therapists, replenish that energy with new pure, channelled energy that is strong and revitalizing. At the same time, because we believe that all physical pain comes from a unhealthy mind, once we have cleared the mind and let the 'garbage energy' coming on to the surface we (the patient and the therapist) can clear it with Reiki, which is so beautiful and grounding.

The first part of 1997 was a great one, I had become extremely successful with my Reiki practice and classes. I decided to close the shop, as, I had had enough. The second part of that year and the beginning of 1998 was a catastrophic year for me and my soul. My mother died at the age of 57. All of a sudden. I had spoken with her that morning and she was fine, by that afternoon at 6pm she had gone. I was distraught, my mother was my inspiration, my muse, I had devoted my Italian life to her, as an Italian mother she had not liked the fact that I had left the nest to go to a foreign country (England) but she used to tell me that she was happy if I was. Having spent most of my life at home with her, had made me understood what an intelligent woman she was and how much love she had put into her children. She loved us so much that she had annulled herself for the sake of her family. She had to put up with a verbally abusive and unfaithful husband. Our family equilibrium had gone forever.

I could not give any more Reiki treatments for more than six months and I was extremely weak and I was getting sick. I would find myself crying for no reason other than grieving for my mother every day. The bereavement lasted for a very long time. When I came out of it I decided to move to America. I felt like I could be of help to people who were dying and their families. I had already had a few experiences of this kind both in England and Italy, and I knew I could have helped people during their transition. Kelly my dearest friend, had been diagnosed with cancer, and I wanted to help her going through the situation.

At the beginning of the 1990s I lived in Paris, working as a translator for an American computer firm. I worked with people from all over the world. I became friends with Kelly, an intelligent girl from New York. We used to talk a lot, getting to know each other, and our friendship grew intimate. Then Kelly went back to US and I returned to London. Kelly and I used to talk at least once a month, telling each other about our experiences and life. Kelly had moved to San Diego, California, where her brother lived.

A few years went by and I was contemplating leaving London for a while to go and live in the US. I did not know where to go or which state to choose from. The reply to my question came suddenly one morning. Kelly called me from Colorado with terrible news; doctors had told that she had cancer of the ovaries. My decision was made; I would go to where Kelly lived to give her all my support and love. So I did. I was very pleased to begin a new life where I did not know anyone but Kelly. As a Reiki Teacher, I am always in search of new experiences that can expand my knowledge and my spiritual path. I have changed my place of residence so many times that I could have spread my Reiki teachings to the four corners of the globe. Arriving in Colorado and meeting Kelly again after so many years gave me a sense of great joy and understanding. At the same time, a stab to my heart at confronting the girl I had met in Paris years before, so full of life and joy; now replaced with the woman before me, defenceless and thin, with long, lifeless grey hair.

Once I moved closer, we used to meet and have long relaxing walks in the Rocky Mountains. Once we took some stale bread and some nuts, and Kelly took me to a forest where there was a colony of prairie dogs that she used to feed daily. It was amazing seeing these wild animals gathering around Kelly when she arrived with food. During our walks, Kelly told me about her life; her difficult relationship with her father who had been verbally abusive for years and her big fear of being with men.

In Reiki we believe that if our mind gives us signals of fear, or fragility, sooner or later our body will experience some kind of turmoil. Kelly was afraid of being with a man and she developed a cancer of the ovaries that had expanded all over her body. I used to give her Reiki often to soothe her pains. Sometimes her ache was so strong that she did not like to be touched. Kelly died on a cold January evening, leaving me with much grief and sadness. But she also left me with the awareness that we should listen to ourselves and our voice within at all times. Kelly also made me promise to reveal her story to the world, so I did.

My life as a Reiki Master has taken me to many places in the world, as I grow as a human being, my life gets enhanced and illuminated. I meet so many interesting people daily and I feel very honoured when some come to me and ask for help or to be with me. I do not know why so many people have chosen me as their Reiki Master, they say they see in me a different light, a different approach. I always say that I am a human being, I make mistakes and I suffer, I have problems like everybody. I have great empathy for the situations people find themselves in that lead to emotional troubles. This is the nature of my mission; helping people who are suffering, helping people to come to term with things, helping people to know Reiki and to meet God. The mission that God has given me and only God can take away from me.

My life's choices, have made me realize that forgiveness is the best way to make peace with yourself and the world around you. I have forgiven myself to have allowed people to interfere so much in my life. If we do not forgive nowadays we cannot progress and if we cannot progress we will not be able to see the transformation of Gaia, mother Earth. In my Reiki centres I receive people from all walks of life, I don't really care who they are as long as they get help, comforting words and energy from the Universe and feel better and enthusiastic about the healing. I always say that only God can heal. If a person comes to seek my help I put them in God's hands. Reiki is a channelling experience. The Reiki practitioner is a go between, between the Source and the client.

Simplicity.

I want simplicity, a lot of it
A meadow, a forest, the smell of fresh flowers and grass
So much simplicity around me … things good and organic

I feel tired of matter, I want to go back to purity
I want to go back to the pure heart inside me
I want to get rid of the toxins inside my body
I want to eat well just the things that grow from Gaia
I don't want to put dead energy inside me anymore…

I want to be myself
I want to go back to stronger life, in good health
I want to go back, to the smile of a child
To the caress of a mother, to the warmth of a father…

I want to go back to smiling at the world,
Back to nature and greet the sun every morning
The moon every evening and the stars every hour of the night

I want to go back to be myself I want to go back
To the wisdom of the soul, to the most beautiful things of my life
To the great and soothing thoughts that cross my mind

I want to go forward and beyond, I want to flow like a tranquil river
That flows into the infinite, towards the most beautiful thing
I want to go back to the brotherhood and sisterhood
To smile at the people and to never, ever be afraid
Of my brothers and sisters in the world

Peace is inside us all, we just need to look for it.
Gaetano vivo

CHAPTER 13

TOUCHED BY LOVE

Frank is a research scientist working in the field of genetics. During the last few years he has been doing post-doctoral work at a large Italian research institute. He feels very lucky to work in a group that is internationally renowned; their research is published in the best scientific journals in the world. He believes that he has the best job in the world; to be a scientist means to have the ability to concretely effect mankind's pursuit of knowledge; therefore, to contribute new clues for interpreting our world.

He had been attending Yoga classes for years, though not very often due to his busy work schedule. I met him at the yoga centre where I was taking part in a Reiki exchange. Our meeting was astounding. Frank was struck with an incredible force by a new vision of a new reality and a new perception of energies. That exchange was Frank's very first experience with Reiki, previously he knew nothing about it and had no idea what to expect. During the meeting he was taken aback by the number of people present who claimed that Reiki had healed their chronic pain issues when pharmaceutical drugs could not.

Frank was utterly fascinated and though during this meeting he received Reiki for just five minutes the physical effects were immediate. All his exhaustion and fatigue were erased in one stroke and replaced by good physical vitality and freshness that were also mental. He undertook further studies with me, Reiki levels 1 and 2.

The first level in particular had a huge impact on his life. He changed home twice, changed positions at work, taking on the additional responsibility of managing people and almost doubled his salary. He was immersed in an extreme state of physical well-being that he had not experienced in years, if ever; the only reason he understood how important it was to invest part of his energies and time to himself was the huge difference with respect to the past.

Reiki made it possible for him to discover this and, at the same time, it provided him with a tool to take action. It is almost as though it awoke forces that had been asleep for a long time and that he had forgotten about; by awakening them, it disrupted patterns that had been stuck for years and replaced them with new ones.

Regrettably, so far he has not had the opportunity of practicing Reiki with others much. He knows that by doing more of this he could refine his sensitivity towards the energies involved in Reiki. This is also the reason why he is putting off taking the third level. It is almost as though he feels the need to 'earn' the right to take part in the class; he cannot do it having practiced only on myself.

The curiosity that surrounds the relationship between science and Reiki, which somewhat follows the issue of the relationship between faith and science, or between science and many other 'non scientific' beliefs, more or less legitimately belongs to historical time frames when science was associated to its results, without realizing how these results were limited to the field of action of the technical instruments at one's disposal.

Today, the general view of science has changed considerably in the eyes of those who practice it, but perhaps very little in the eyes of lay people. Perhaps a scientist is still regarded as a sceptic who needs to find a logical explanation for everything. Modern scientists are aware of the fact that science is a method that is not identical to its results that in fact are always changing and are never definitive. To be believers or skeptics when dealing with a phenomenon in either case is prejudicial, and this is incompatible with a scientific approach that must be neutral. Often, there is a tendency to forget that science is made by man and that it avails itself of tools, albeit very powerful ones, that are an extension of human senses or of the senses that one can be aware of; after all, by definition, science cannot transcend man, therefore it cannot transcend human limitations.

There are those who believe that man is limitless and that the universe and its phenomena are entirely within human grasp. This attitude is very reminiscent of pre-Copernican stances, with man at the centre of the universe, as in pre-scientific times. In summary, Frank feels that in following a scientific approach, man can explore only a certain portion of the phenomena that pertain to the universe, others he may well perceive, but he will only be able to explore when appropriate tools are available; finally, there are others, perhaps the greatest part that man will never perceive at all. Personally, Frank says he believes that it is a poor scientist who forgets this and decides to adopt an attitude of arrogance or prejudice towards something he cannot understand, or for which he cannot understand the underlying mechanisms.

Getting back to Reiki, if a scientist is drawn to it out of curiosity, the most sensible thing (if not the only thing) to do is to try it out and see what happens. To label it or not then becomes a matter of personal choice; but this, as Frank mentioned before, is outside the realm of science. As far as he is concerned, all that he has learned from direct experience is that Reiki is a wonderful gift both selfishly and for others. He appreciates the lack of dogmas and overtones in Reiki. The only thing that you can do with Reiki is practice it and, if it works, all the better. It is working for Frank and he considers himself very fortunate indeed: whatever the underlying mechanisms, he has a wonderful tool at his disposal to ensure his physical and spiritual well-being.

Now I come to telling you of John who I met in Milan in 2005. He was looking for clarity in his life. John had met a Reiki Master in Milan, years before and he had learned Reiki level I with him with little result. He also knew that many people had used and abused Reiki for their own purposes so he was very disillusioned about it all. He had heard of me through many of his friends and felt he had to meet me. So when we first met John was filled with a mixture of curiosity and scepticism. This was heightened by the fact that prior to our meeting he had been told that not only was I a Reiki Master, but I had the ability to communicate with angelic and other ethereal beings.

We met at the home of a pupil of mine. John had no idea what to ask me, he seemed really confused. Nonetheless, he soon found his voice and told me about his concerns about Reiki. I agreed that I too had found Reiki had become a 'commodity' in Italy. During my time away Reiki as I saw it now had lost its true worth in Italy, and it was my aim to restore a bit of truth to this form of healing. I explained to John that Reiki is just another manifestation of 'love'. I knew of other teachers in Italy who were also now working to teach and spread the word about Reiki, that it is only love. John was not sure if he should quit and look for other things or if he should have continued to learn more about Reiki. He said he had not found as much candour in other people, who described themselves as the custodians of knowledge and teachers of healing techniques.

Suddenly a stone on the table caught John's eye. I looked at him and asked him to pick it up, hold it and remain silent for few minutes just listening. After a little while I asked John to tell him what he could hear. He said he felt a little unsure to start with and so didn't hear anything, but then all of a sudden, as he began to relax, a wave of energy rippled through his entire body. John told me that the first thing was just sounds that seemed to come from afar, it was like day dreaming, then he heard children in the distance. John said he felt joy and love and he started to shed tears of joy. John said he could feel a joyful, playful spirit dancing around him. He said he had no idea of what he was saying, in that moment.

John had heard of such experiences before but he knew that you had to be very relaxed and in a deep meditation. I told him that, the stone he was holding was very rare and carried the energy of Lemuria, the ancient lost continent, whose inhabitants were in contact with the souls of the Pleiades constellation. John said that what struck him most was the ease and sincerity with which I gave him this information. Normally he was very sceptical about these types of experiences, which always seemed to be some kind of trick or illusion. But the quality of the experience he had with me was completely different from all his previous ones.

I could not scientifically prove to John where the stone had come from or the energy and knowledge it carried, but it was enough for him to 'feel' this as a truth. He said it was a new experience for him and that the information he had received was through his heart, not through the rational or emotional mind. I told him that these were also new experiences for me, but that I did believe we were evolving through spiritual messages like this. Since then John has often thought back to that experience, or rather he has tried to re-live it. In many ways John says he feels more open and clear with himself and with people at work, in everyday life. It is as if a door had been opened for him on that day.

CHAPTER 14

THE INFINITE (REIKI & THE ANGELS)

After a recent Reiki level 1 session I came to a most amazing understanding that beautifully unified my long-term experiences of Reiki and my more recent revelations care of the Angels of Transparency. They spoke to me and said, 'You are looking? What are you looking for; you need to go beyond your minds towards the unknown, towards the infinite. We are here to help others who are not in the light yet, and first of all you need to help yourselves. When you have healed, then you will be able to assist others to have a different view of the world. Remember, beloved ones, that *love* is what you need to have in your hearts always, love is what helps you to go forward in life. Only with love we can fight battles and win wars. Those internal battles and those big and external battles, only in this way, opening the heart and listening to us will you be able to achieve peace inside and worldwide peace

Don't judge others, don't analyze every little thing, let it be, let it go, leave your mind going beyond let it go and do not think, as if you want positive energies and positive thinking always flows inside you. You will become more beautiful after the Reiki initiations; observe what people say about the way you appear to them. Don't let anyone spoil this gift; you are filled with love now. Love must reign and not judgmental actions, nor the frustrations of your daily life, not what the mind tells us, this all belong to the past, as from now on you will talk with your heart, only speaking from the heart will you win. Don't look behind you anymore, only look before you, with this new light in your heart you will give a new sense at your life. With a different light in your heart, you will give a sense to your life, to your hopes, to the nature, to the trees, to the plants and the flower, to all that is wonderful and surround us. God be with you always blessed ones'.

In a Channelling with Archangel Metatron, regarding the new symbols coming through, like Xantia, I asked if he could elaborate on them and their significance. Metatron replied, 'This is the language of sacred geometry. Those sacred symbols are esoteric maps... There are 144,000 coming at this time, which is like a huge jigsaw puzzle and each of these 144,000 pieces are bringing together an energy that is assisting the shift of Mother Earth and of the consciousness of Humanity as a completion of the souls. This shift to be referred to as the domino effect, the syndrome of the 100 monkeys, when enough come together, then the energy and dynamics change and it changes in many levels including, genetically. It is the mass mind that lots of people on the planet would like to ignore, but it is why one invention may be invented by the same people at the same time, because when you get the 144,000 together the puzzle is together and the shift can be made, and all that is happening in that shift, including the genetic makeup, will be shifted and moved in the huge quantum leap that is beyond the human language.'

Each of us will be imprinted in the geometric symbols. It would be like having one symbol coming into our DNA telling us about ourselves and about our being, we will then learn from this master and get that knowledge. And each one of us can get on more than one, up to 12 symbols, or master symbols and the information being imprinted on the DNA, getting light which is information, and as we progress we get more symbols, no more that 12 at time, shifting, learning, bringing in frequencies higher and higher in a form of school. These symbols are not like the one you would find on a piece of paper, they are much more, they are living symbols, they are pathways, but they are also the living aspects or beings that have actually moved in to a reality that that symbol is. These are living symbols that will become a part of a living organism to accelerate at a greater and greater speed and be able to be at such high vibration that they can handle a greater and greater aspect of light of knowledge. Language is limiting to explain what this is.

Now I am working at a programme which is called Transformational Healing Evolution (T.H.E), which includes many of the modalities I have learned in my long researches for illumination. Through the teachings of Metatron and Michael, they have asked me to take people slowly by hands and easily show them the beauty of the universe. To comprehend the way to listen to the angels and feel their presence around us. Communicate with them, to never be afraid of what we are going to touch or experimenting, because we are transforming and the planet with us. We are becoming all beings of light and highly spiritual and attuned to the Universal Energy. They are showing us the different approaches and methodologies to enhance people's lives. They are telling us, that daily, we should plant a seed in the heart of those people who are less aware of the energy, this seed that would allow them to understand the transformation that the Planet is going through. Not to stop at the superficiality of the matter, at the surface of the subject, but going deeper and really feel the planet in their heart as their own, and feel a sense of great joy and love towards it.

KA KITE ANŌ (SEE YOU AGAIN)

My name is Nooria, I teach English in Milan, Italy, but I'm originally from New Zealand. My grandmother was Maori and my
grandfather was Chinese. This was a powerful combination
which I believe is at the heart of my interest in the spirit world
and the energies of the natural world. When I was little I lived
with my grandparents and I remember my Nena (grandmother)
used to touch people's bodies to heal them and say things that
sounded very ritualistic. I healed from a gaping wound after my
Nena had touched me.

My uncle, my mother's brother, was a Maori *Tohunga*
(medicine man or shaman) and also healed people with the touch
of his hands. The Maori people are close to the energy of Earth
and Nature and I feel inside me there is a Maori warrior that
comes out when I most need it. I must fight in this life. I believe
that there is karma, the law of cause and effect, which allows us
to relive and complete the experiences of past lives. I believe that
with death our spirit goes on living. Since I was little, I felt the
existence of this spiritual reality and of these energies and I
realized that we cannot know why certain things happen at a
certain time, in a certain way.

I believe that when we are born, our body is a perfect
mechanism that we slowly destroy during our life time. We must
look after and continually heal our metaphysical and psychological being, because if we don't then our physical body will get
sick. All of us know deep down how to use these energies well,
but we forget during our busy lives that is why there are certain
chosen people that teach us how to heal our body and mind.

I met Gaetano Vivo in London a few years ago and was taught

Reiki by him. I have been doing that on myself and on some friends and family. I use Reiki now on myself a lot because I am ill. First I had breast cancer, then brain cancer. I have performed Reiki on myself during the time surrounding my brain operation, both before and after the actual operation in 2005. The other patients in the hospital wanted painkillers, I did not feel any pain. I know Reiki was giving me strength and healing from the pain. The doctors in the hospital were very surprised, asked me what was I doing and when I explained it to them only one nurse knew anything about it.

During a Reiki session, I usually listen to relaxation music and work a lot with visualization. I felt ready for the operation and I went in smiling and relaxed. I have come out of this experience stronger and wiser. I was also speaking about my experience to the old lady in the bed next to mine, she needed strength and support. It was not yet my time to die, evidently I still needed to do things.

Reiki has played a very important role in this experience. For me Reiki is an Energy that gave me the strength I needed to go forward. People need to understand that it is 'love' that we need the most, and nothing else and we need to cherish that love in order to give it to ourselves and others. Reiki is giving me the courage and the strength to fight, to live and to love. I am always Nooria, I am always the same. I have an illness but I do always the same things and if I get tired I stop and thank the Energy of having given more strength. This strength I am sure comes from Reiki.

Reiki, this universal energy, this love is a very powerful tool and perhaps it is the same healing power that has inspired great legendary tales of healing among the ancient peoples of this world and during Jesus' lifetime. It is not a personal power. It is the strength of life that comes from deep within our very being. Nothing is impossible; but we need to have faith, a belief to heal. You need to believe you can rise above your ill-feelings, if you believe instead that you are the victim then you will become the victim… may you always choose to be the warrior.

ACKNOWLEDGEMENTS

I am grateful to life and to the Great Spirit for their gifts that in their simplicity are powerful and give joy and hope. I am also grateful to my students, everywhere for sharing their knowledge through their testimonies; out of respect for their privacy their names have been changed.

A great 'thank you' to Sally and Sophie Pullinger, in Glastonbury. Sally's channel, Chung Fu, is one of my teachers and has shown me the way to heal my inner child whose story is written in these pages. I am forever grateful to you both for your great love and support. I thank Mr Stefano Fusi, who has helped me to best deliver the often deep and life-enhancing channellings. Thanks to Prof Dr Damaso Caprioglio, whose testimonial on the beauty and power of Reiki will enhance people's love for this powerfully loving ancient Japanese healing art.

I want to thank Kate Osborne, my agent in the UK, who since the beginning of this project, believed, encouraged and supported me all along with friendship, harmony and great love for the angels and the channelling that they are giving us these days. I want to also thank my Press Office in Italy, Patrizia and Laura Gucciardo, for helping me break through the very difficult Italian Catholic market with great success and great courage.

Finally to all my friends and family whose constant support, love and respect for my work propels me forward in my life mission.

ABOUT THE AUTHOR

Gaetano Vivo is a Reiki Master, practicing in the UK, the US and Italy. As well as being a fully-qualified and advanced practitioner of Reiki, he is a member of the Complementary Medical Association of Great Britain, the International Council of Holistic Therapies, the International Association of Reiki Professionals, and a member of the Noetic Association of America. In over 10 years practising this therapy, Gaetano has treated many hundreds of clients from all walks of life.

Gaetano became a Reiki Master following a turning point in his life. He ran a bookshop (The Metaphysical Centre) and people commented on how relaxing they found his presence. He initially experienced Reiki from a ten minute taster session and then from that point on it was as if a gate had opened in his life and he decided to learn more about Reiki. When his training was sufficiently advanced he began offering his staff treatments and then set up his clinic.

Gaetano is the author of the popular *Reiki is Love* published by Booksurge, 2006 collection of case studies aimed at the UK/US market, and two other books on Reiki for Italian audiences.

Reiki is one of many healing therapies he practises; others include Vibrational Psychic Surgery, Crystal Therapy and Karuna Reiki Treatments. In addition to treating clients Gaetano also instructs students in the art of Reiki.

AXIS MUNDI
BOOKS

Axis Mundi Books provide the most revealing and coherent
explorations and investigations of the world of hidden or
forbidden knowledge. Take a fascinating journey into the realm
of Esoteric Mysteries, Magic, Mysticism, Angels, Cosmology,
Alchemy, Gnosticism, Theosophy, Kabbalah, Secret Societies and
Religions, Symbolism, Quantum Theory, Apocalyptic
Mythology, Holy Grail and Alternative Views of Mainstream
Religion.